GOYA'S P

GOYA'S PRINTS

The Tomás Harris Collection in the British Museum

Juliet Wilson-Bareau

Published for the Trustees of the British Museum
by British Museum Press

In memory of Tomás,

Violeta and Conchita,

and for Enriqueta

© 1981 The Trustees of the British Museum

Published by British Museum Press
A division of The British Museum Company Ltd
46 Bloomsbury Street, London WC1B 3QQ

First published 1981
Reprinted, with revisions, 1996

British Library Cataloguing in Publication Data
Wilson-Bareau, Juliet
  Goya's prints.
  1. Goya, Francisco de
  I. Title   II. Goya, Francisco de
  769.92′4   NE702.G/

ISBN 0–7141–0789–1

Set in 11/12 Van Dijck
and printed in Great Britain by
BAS Printers, Over Wallop, Hampshire

Frontispiece *The sleep of reason produces monsters*
(*Caprichos* Plate 43)

Contents

P. 1

Fran.co Goya y Lucientes
Pintor.

1 Francisco Goya y Lucientes, Painter (*Caprichos* Plate 1)

Preface

The immediate purpose of this book, and of the exhibition which it accompanies, is to commemorate one of the most important acquisitions made by the Department of Prints and Drawings since the last war. The famous collection of Goya's prints formed by the late Tomás Harris was accepted in lieu of duty on his estate and that of his wife by H.M. Treasury and formally transferred to the British Museum in 1979. The range and scope of the collection is discussed fully in the last section of this book, but it can be claimed that the Department now has numerically the largest Goya collection in the world, and one which has few rivals in importance. The Department is therefore very much in the debt of Tomás Harris, who had always intended that his collection should find a home in the Museum where he had deposited it on loan before his untimely death in 1964, and of those who have ensured that his wishes have been fulfilled. Foremost among these are his three sisters, Miss Violeta Harris, Mrs Conchita Wolff and Mrs Enriqueta Frankfort, to whom the Department is also grateful for the loan of three proofs of the *Caprichos*.

The present book is the work of Juliet Wilson Bareau, who was Tomás Harris's assistant in the preparation of his standard catalogue of Goya's prints and herself an authority on Goya. She was invited to write a handbook which, without a daunting apparatus of scholarly references, would provide the non-specialist interested in Goya and his period with an up-to-date account of the artist's life and work as a printmaker. She wishes me to express her thanks for their unfailing help and encouragement to Professor Nigel Glendinning of Queen Mary College, London University, and to Antony Griffiths of the Department of Prints and Drawings who has been responsible for the organisation of the exhibition.

The many friends and colleagues whom she would also like to acknowledge will find their names in the bibliography which replaces footnote references and provides the general reader with a guide to the literature, more particularly related to Goya's prints, on which this book is based.

The note on the Goya collection in the British Museum and the checklist of Goya's prints and drawings in the Department have been compiled by Antony Griffiths. All the illustrations are of works in the British Museum, with the exception of the last two plates which belong to a private collection and to the Museum of Fine Arts at Boston and which are reproduced by kind permission of their respective owners. Works in the British Museum have been specially photographed for this book by Graham Javes and Ivor Kerslake of the Photographic Service.

J. A. GERE
Keeper, Department of Prints and Drawings

A man must be born endowed with a rare, inventive talent,
have had a wide experience of life and have plumbed the depths
of the human heart in order . . . to compose satires like these.

Gregorio González Azaola, 'Sátiras de Goya', *Semanario Patriótico*,
Cadiz, March 1811

This survey of Goya's activity as a printmaker first appeared in 1981, nearly twenty years after the publication of Tomás Harris's monumental catalogue in 1964. More than three decades have now passed since that date, and Harris's catalogue has not been updated or replaced. However, a great deal of research has of course been carried out during this long period and many discoveries have been made. Changes to the chronology have been proposed for several groups of etchings and lithographs; hitherto unknown proofs have appeared and new states have been identified, while in the case of a preparatory drawing for the *Tauromaquia* (Harris 247a) the missing print itself has come to light. Perhaps Harris's most original and far-reaching contribution was his concern to catalogue not simply the 'rarities', the early proofs taken in the course of the artist's work and up to the printing of an edition, but to identify the distinctive characteristics of the very large number of editions that were taken from Goya's original copperplates. Here, too, fresh documentation concerning the printing of the editions in the Calcografía Nacional in Madrid is currently being 'matched' with the physical characteristics of the growing quantities of papers and bindings that do not accord with the descriptions in Harris's otherwise remarkably complete catalogue.

The time is certainly ripe for a Goya print catalogue that will take account of all the new thinking and new material. Meanwhile, since recent research into Goya's prints is to be found in a multiplicity of forms – articles and conference papers, exhibition and dealers' catalogues – that are not easily available to the general reader, and are couched in a variety of languages, it seems appropriate to republish this brief but useful survey which has been in constant demand since it first appeared. The field of Goya studies is a particularly vigorous one and the importance of the prints in assessing the whole of the artist's oeuvre cannot be overstated. Juliet Wilson-Bareau's text remains the most accessible introduction to this complex subject.

ANTONY GRIFFITHS
Keeper, Department of Prints and Drawings

1 Goya and his Time

Francisco Goya y Lucientes was born near Saragossa in the province of Aragon in 1746, the year in which the Bourbon king Ferdinand VI succeeded to the throne of Spain. He studied under a respected local artist who had trained in Naples, but he failed to win a vote in competitions at the Academy of San Fernando in Madrid in 1764 and 1766. Undaunted, Goya went off to Rome to continue his studies there 'at his own expense'. After some early successes in Saragossa following his return in 1771 he was, again in his own words, 'called by don Antonio Rafael de Mengs' to Madrid to work on designs for the Royal Tapestry Factory. He rose from these humble beginnings to become the most celebrated painter of his day, both for his portraits and for his original compositions. He became Director of Painting at the Academy and rose to the position of First Court Painter to Charles IV and María Luisa in 1799, the year in which he published the set of prints entitled *Los Caprichos*. Thereafter, partly as a result of the Napoleonic war and the political situation, he received fewer official commissions and devoted much of his time to his own private work in painting, drawing and printmaking. He died in Bordeaux in 1828 at the age of eighty-two.

Goya's life spanned one of the most complex and interesting periods in history, and his art was profoundly affected by the events through which he lived. During the reigns of the Bourbon kings Ferdinand VI and particularly Charles III, Italian and French influences were very strong at the Spanish court and the most prestigious foreign artists were employed on important projects including the building and decoration of the new Royal Palace in Madrid, after the catastrophic destruction of the old Alcázar by fire in 1734. The French artists favoured by the first of the Bourbons largely gave way to Italians under Ferdinand VI and Charles III, although French influence remained very strong. Then, in the 1760s, the German neo-classical artist Anton Raffael Mengs, followed by Giovanni Battista Tiepolo, the last of the great Italian rococo artists, were invited to Madrid to work on decorations for the royal palaces.

As part of the policies of centralisation and reorganisation, a Royal Academy of Fine Arts was established under Ferdinand VI and Spanish artists, mostly trained in Rome, gradually took over from the foreigners. After the French painter Louis Michel van Loo and the Neapolitan Corrado Giaquinto, Spanish artists such as Antonio González Velázquez, then Francisco Bayeu and Maella, followed by Goya and Camarón were all appointed Professors of Painting at the Academy and all held the post of Court Painter. Goya's nomination took place in 1789, the year of the coronation of Charles IV and María Luisa of whom he painted numerous official portraits. This was also the year of the French Revolution and the start of an extremely complex period in Spanish politics, influenced as much by external affairs as by the rise and fall of ministers and favourites, chief among them the queen's lover, Manuel Godoy. In a period of political turmoil and sordid personal intrigue, satire and caricature were the weapons of the liberal intellectuals – poets, playwrights and pamphleteers – who were deeply affected by the ideals of the Enlightenment. It was in this context that Goya's *Caprichos* were created.

The constant undermining of responsible government and the collapse of morals at the court led to riots and plots against the favourite in the years around the turn of the century, and ultimately to the forced abdication of Charles IV. With the arrival of Napoleon's troops in 1808, his brother Joseph Bonaparte was installed on the throne and the people of Spain rose in violent revolt against the foreign invaders. The five years of war and terrible famine were recorded in Goya's etchings made between 1810 and 1813, the year in which the French were finally expelled after Wellington's victory at Vitoria. A year later, Goya painted his great canvases commemorating the uprising and executions of 2 and 3 May 1808 in Madrid.

Once freed from the French invaders, Spain fell subject to the reaction of Ferdinand VII, a ruthless tyrant who had plotted with Napoleon against Godoy and who now did all he could to root out and destroy the liberal Constitution and the ideals which had been introduced into Spain through the efforts of Goya's enlightened friends. Ferdinand's reign of terror is reflected in the later plates which Goya added to the war scenes in the series later published as *The Disasters of War*. The 'black paintings' originally on the walls of his house on the outskirts of Madrid (now in the Prado), and an enigmatic series of prints known as the *Disparates* or *Proverbios* also belong to this dark and dangerous period.

Goya was now old, ill and isolated. After the intervention of the French and the end of three years of constitutional government in 1823, he went into hiding for several months. His liberal friends were dead, imprisoned or in exile and Goya chose to leave Spain and settle in Bordeaux. Despite his restless, impatient nature, his great age and his infirmities, four years of peace resulted in a final, magnificent outburst of activity – portraits, miniature paintings of a totally unconventional kind, innumerable drawings of breathtaking vitality, and a remarkable series of lithographs. This included the four great *Bulls of Bordeaux* which the virtually unknown exile, in his eightieth year, launched on to the French market at the same time as the young Delacroix was copying figures from his *Caprichos* published a quarter-century before.

Prints and printmaking played a vital role throughout Goya's career. In a brief autobiographical note published in 1828, the year of his death, he described his training in the 1760s as 'a pupil of don José Luzán in Saragossa, who taught him the principles of drawing, making him copy the best prints that he had'. This was the accepted method of teaching at that time, but Goya insisted that 'he had no other teacher than his own observation of the characteristics of the celebrated painters and paintings in Rome and in Spain'. In a slightly longer note written a few years later, Goya's son Xavier offered the additional information that his father 'looked with veneration at Velasquez and Rembrandt but above all he studied and looked at Nature whom he called his mistress'.

Goya, however, certainly studied prints with profit and enjoyment, and by 1812 he owned a sizeable collection including 'ten by Rembrandt' and 'a collection by Piranesi'. Many of his friends and colleagues were print collectors and the Academy of Fine Arts in Madrid built up an impressive study collection of prints and illustrated books in the years following its inauguration in 1752.

In the eighteenth century all artists depended on reproductive prints (as sculptors depended on casts) for their knowledge and understanding of the paintings and drawings of the acknowledged masters whose work they had no other opportunity of seeing. The standard methods of printmaking were engraving and etching. Engraving was the older of the two. The process involves incising the lines of a design into a copper plate with a v-shaped tool called a burin. The plate, when completed, is covered with ink which is carefully wiped away so as to clean the surface, leaving ink only in the engraved lines. The image is printed by covering the plate with a sheet of paper and running it through a roller press (similar to the household mangle) so that the ink transfers to the paper. The second process, etching, is a variant which involves the use of acid to eat the lines of the design into the plate. The copper is first covered with a ground – a layer of resin or wax which is impermeable. Into this the design is drawn with a needle so as to expose the copper. The plate is placed in a bath of acid until the lines are sufficiently bitten; the ground is then cleaned off, and the plate printed in the same way as an engraving. In the eighteenth century the tendency was for engraving, a laborious and highly skilled process, to be used by professional printmaker craftsmen to make reproductions of paintings in a rather uniform and often academic manner. Etching, by contrast, requires no professional apprenticeship, and was often used by painters (for example Rembrandt and Tiepolo) in highly individual ways to create compositions that were as original as their drawings.

Before Goya, there was virtually no tradition of original printmaking in Spain. Etching and engraving were mainly practised in the later seventeenth and throughout the eighteenth centuries, to satisfy an increasing demand for religious images, topographical and reproductive prints, illustrations for books and instructive manuals, as well as prints documenting costumes, trades and pastimes. The influx of foreign prints – French, Flemish and Italian – in the first half of the eighteenth century was viewed with alarm and despondency by those who wished to raise the status and quality of the arts in Spain.

When the Academy of Fine Arts of San Fernando was established in Madrid in 1752, the teaching of printmaking was added to that of the 'three noble arts' of architecture, sculpture and painting. One of its first acts was to send promising students to Paris, the unchallenged centre of printmaking in Europe. The most outstanding of these was Manuel Salvador Carmona who returned to Madrid in 1763 and formed a school of expert engravers whose avowed purpose was to contribute to the education and enlightenment of the Spanish people and to the propagation of Spanish culture and achievements abroad. These engravers produced a steady stream of maps and plans, historical and documentary prints, portraits of Spain's rulers and great men, depictions of her finest buildings and monuments and copies of the celebrated works of art by Spanish and foreign artists in the great royal and ecclesiastical collections.

In 1761, two years after the accession of Charles III who was himself an enthusiastic etcher, a remarkably complete and detailed little handbook on engraving was published in Madrid. Don Manuel de Rueda, an expert amateur printmaker (who held an administrative post in the Royal Artillery), dedicated his 'Instruction for engraving on copper . . . in burin, etching and mezzotint . . .' to the Royal Academy of San Fernando, expressing the hope that it would prove 'useful to the Professors of Engraving' and extolling the particular virtues of etching as a rapid method of reproducing 'the appearance of every visible thing' for the instruction and enjoyment of the public.

In 1789 Carmona persuaded Charles III to set up a Royal Chalcography to provide printing facilities and to build up a national stock of engraved plates on the model of the French 'Cabinet du Roi' and the Papal Chalcography in Rome. It was to this institution that Goya handed over the plates of his *Caprichos* in 1803, by which time over two and a half thousand engraved plates were in its possession. In later years almost all of Goya's plates were acquired by the Calcografía Nacional, as it came to be called, and editions from them have been regularly printed since the middle of the nineteenth century.

Some of Goya's earliest paintings were directly based on prints after Simon Vouet and

Carlo Maratta and in his later work prints provided many other sources of inspiration. His own pictures were reproduced by some of the best Spanish engravers. He also made portrait drawings for engravings by Carmona and his pupil Selma, and a commemorative design, executed by the French engraver Pierre Philippe Choffard. He even drew a lively scene to illustrate the Madrid Academy's great 1780 edition of *Don Quixote*, but although it was engraved, the plate, for unknown reasons, was not included in the publication. Goya made many further drawings which were never engraved or of which no impressions have survived. The most important single project was the series of portraits intended to illustrate the great historical dictionary of Spanish artists compiled by his friend Juan Agustín Ceán Bermúdez, which was published, without illustrations, in 1800.

These illustrations and portraits were only a minor aspect of Goya's preoccupation with the art of printmaking. In the course of his long career he made nearly three hundred prints, most of them entirely original compositions, and to the freedom and spontaneity of etching he soon added the tonal and painterly qualities of aquatint, a process which had been invented in the 1760s and which only came into general use in the 1770s and 1780s. Whereas etching uses an impermeable ground, aquatint relies on a ground of discreet grains of resin. Around these the acid bites in tiny 'pools' to create areas of tone; areas to be left white are simply stopped out with a varnish that prevents the acid from reaching the copper. Still experimenting at the end of his life, he took up

90 the new technique of lithography, trying it out in 1819, the year it was introduced into
94–5 Spain, and developing his use of it in Bordeaux six years later to create the *Bulls of Bordeaux*, which in the audacity of their use of the medium have never been surpassed.

None of Goya's great series of prints was commissioned, and throughout his career he always emphasised his status as a painter, as well as insisting on the originality of his
7–10 compositions. Even his copies after Velasquez were remarkably original works in their own right, which conveyed the atmosphere and quality of Velasquez's painting in a way that no literal transcription could.

The etching of the eighty plates of the *Caprichos*, published in an edition of three hundred copies, was undertaken by Goya as his contribution to the campaign being waged by his liberal friends to bring the Enlightenment to Spain, a battle in which he had many personal reasons for being involved. Many of the plates refer to individuals at the Spanish court whom he would have known well as the result of his position as Court Painter. The later *caprichos enfáticos* which conclude the series of the *Disasters of War*, and possibly the obscure *Disparates* of the same period, were also made with a strong sense of commitment to his own and his friends' liberal ideas. Even the *Tauromaquia*, devoted to an apparently anodyne account of the history and development of bullfighting, may contain critical and philosophical ideas. The series of prints showing 'the fatal consequences of Spain's bloody war with Bonaparte' displays a very direct response to the events of the time, although its expansion to include the satirical *caprichos enfáticos* made publication impossible, and the prints did not appear until the Academy issued them in 1863. The greater part of Goya's print production was therefore a direct and personal response to his involvement in the ideas and events of his time, which gives it a seriousness and significance quite unprecedented and perhaps unparalleled in the work of any other printmaker.

2 The Early Prints

Goya's earliest prints are three etchings of religious subjects. His first known essay, a

2 little *Flight into Egypt*, would be unrecognisable as his work if he had not added his name to the plate. Although the image appears naïve and conventional and the etching style is very simple, there is a sense of gravity and naturalness in the heavily robed figures which recalls the impressive mural cycle painted by the young Goya for a monastery near Saragossa in 1774, three years after his return from Rome. In the previous year, at the age of twenty-seven, Goya had married the sister of Francisco Bayeu, the influential artist trained by Mengs, who was established in Madrid as Court Painter and professor of painting at the Academy, and it is tempting to imagine that the *Flight into Egypt*, of which only seven impressions are known, may have been etched to celebrate the birth of the young couple's first child, a son, in 1774.

Following Mengs's return to Spain that same year, Goya and Josefa went to live with the Bayeu family in Madrid. Tomás Harris suggested that a little print of exactly the

3-4 same size as the *Flight*, representing the Italian hermit San Francesco di Paola, may have been made to commemorate the birth of a fourth son, who was christened Francisco de Paula Antonio Benito in August 1780. This second print shows a remarkable development in Goya's approach and handling of the etching medium. In the *Flight* the natural style and simple neo-classical figures have some affinity with the first tapestry designs which Goya made under his brother-in-law's supervision in 1775. But the *San Francisco de Paula* of some six years later evidently owes a great deal to the influence of the Tiepolo family who were in Madrid until 1770.

As Court Painter, Francisco Bayeu must have been in close contact with the Tiepolo family. His print collection included many etchings by Domenico Tiepolo, including the *Raccolta di Teste* (Collection of Heads), published in Venice in 1774–5. Domenico himself (whose brother Lorenzo remained in Madrid after his return to Italy in 1770) owned most of Goya's early prints, as well as a copy of the *Caprichos* which appeared in 1799, five years before his death. Goya's *San Francisco* has often been compared with the *Teste* of Domenico and with his father Giambattista's little *Saint Joseph*, although the emotional intensity of Goya's saint is entirely Spanish. The print may also owe something to the influence of Rembrandt, perhaps through the prints of the Genoese artist Castiglione. The interplay of the flickering etched line and the warm luminosity of the paper is characteristic of most of Goya's early prints and confirms his development away from the disciplined style of academic engraving towards a highly personal use of the etching medium.

Goya's prints were all based on preparatory drawings. Two of the earliest were made by a method described in Rueda's handbook: the back of the drawing was covered with chalk, laid against the grounded plate and the design transferred by drawing over the lines with a stylus so that the chalk adhered to the ground. This was the case with the print of *San Francisco* (the drawing, lost during the Civil War, is known from a

5-6 photograph) and with the *Garrotted man*. Rueda pointed out the inconvenience of this

2 *The Flight into Egypt*

3–4 *San Francisco de Paula*. Before and after correction of 'CARI'

method because it reverses the design of the drawing. In Goya's etching the saint holds

3 his stick in his left hand, and in the two proofs of the first state the letters CARI (for Caritas, the saint's device) print the wrong way round. The plate was re-etched to

4 correct the mistake and further alterations to the figure of the saint, indicated in pen on the British Museum proof and in chalk on the second proof in the Bibliothèque Nationale, were carried out with the drypoint (a sharp needle scratched directly into the plate) and with the burin of the professional engraver. Correcting and reworking an etched copperplate is to some extent a hazardous business since the plate has to be regrounded and reimmersed in the acid bath. In the case of a third early print representing San Isidro, the patron saint of Madrid, which is only known in one impression, the first etching was a failure and the plate was presumably destroyed in attempts to rework it. This plate does, however, mark an advance in that a more sophisticated method was used to transfer the design to the plate. The drawing was damped and placed face down against the grounded plate. By running the two together through a press, the design was transferred in reverse so that the print taken from the plate appears in the same sense as the original drawing. This method was henceforth used by Goya in almost all his plates, as can be seen from the indentations of the plate on many of the drawings.

In the later 1770s Goya produced a print of extraordinary originality showing a victim

6 of the Spanish form of death by garrotting. The dead man, a gentleman criminal who could claim this nobler form of capital punishment in place of hanging, is seated on the block, his neck encircled by the iron ring which has strangled him. A candle burning at his side casts arbitrary shadows which increase the pathos of the scene. The intensity

5 already felt in the *San Francisco* is here carried much further. Both the drawing in the British Museum, which is incised for transfer, and the print succeed in conveying an overwhelming impression of suffering and death. The face, originally etched in the delicate manner of the (now faded) drawing, was later 'battered' with an engraving tool to blunt the precision of the fine lines and increase the tragic sense of destruction in the sagging features. Because the lines of the long, unbound hair were too closely laid and broke down in the biting of the plate, Goya re-etched this area, accidentally causing two lines of 'foul biting'. As the plate wears in later editions the rework in the head stands out very clearly.

Why Goya should have etched and printed this presumably unsaleable subject is unknown. If it had been intended to represent a well-known criminal, he would have added an engraved inscription. Rather it seems to be the record of his first confrontation with the kind of violence and brutality – far removed from the brawls and quarrels of the tapestry cartoons – which were to reappear in the *Caprichos* and above all in the etchings of *Prisoners* and some of the most pathetic scenes of the *Disasters of War* made thirty-five years later. This print reveals already the mature Goya and has long been regarded as one of his archetypal images. It was copied in paintings by Romantic artists, it was reproduced in facsimiles and deceptive copies, and the original copperplate was reprinted in the Calcografía long after it was worn out.

In April 1778, Goya completed the largest tapestry cartoon he ever painted. The Director of the Royal Tapestry Factory described it as representing the Plazuela de la Cebada in Madrid and Goya's invoice gives an extremely detailed account of the scene showing 'a blind man singing to his guitar with his *lazarillo* [boy guide] and fourteen

11 figures listening to him . . .'. Goya's rare and attractive print is the largest that he ever etched and the only reproduction he ever made of one of his paintings. It shows the tapestry cartoon perhaps not exactly as Goya originally painted it, but certainly before it was altered by him later that year because the weavers found it impossible to interpret.

5 Drawing for *The garrotted man*

6 *The garrotted man*

In its final version, the cartoon was simplified and the huge expanse of sky and cloud which would have been particularly difficult to weave was partially filled with conventional trees and foliage.

Compared with the decorative, essentially trivial compositions of most of his colleagues working for the tapestry factory, Goya painted taut little dramas and comedies, in the manner of Ramón de la Cruz's highly popular theatrical sketches where the characters are given a real existence and *raison d'être* by their life-like and expressive relationships to each other. Goya's etching after his tapestry cartoon is far from the stilted, descriptive prints of Spanish costumes and manners which were beginning to enjoy wide popularity, and from the French taste of the court; it has much more in common, in the straightforward unity of its composition, with the works of the Tiepolos and of Velasquez, whose paintings he was intently studying at this time at the Royal Palace.

In 1769, thirty-five years after the destruction of the Alcázar, the great Palacio Nuevo, with its fresco decorations by Giaquinto, Tiepolo and Mengs, was at last ready for occupation. Charles III, wishing to make it as splendid as Versailles, brought together the best pictures in the royal collections for display in the various state apartments and royal chambers. By 1772, when an inventory was made, 981 paintings were already hanging in the rooms.

The royal palace and its collections were seen by increasing numbers of visitors and excited considerable interest. Ceán Bermúdez, the art historian and friend of Goya, had trained as an artist himself in Seville and noted that when his old teacher finally saw the great paintings in the palaces in and near Madrid, he bitterly regretted not having known them in his youth. In 1776 Antonio Ponz, another artist turned art historian, published his description of Madrid as part of a series entitled *Viage de España* (Travels in Spain). It was full of up-to-date information (even mentioning the latest designs for tapestries being painted by Goya and his colleagues) and described in detail the treasures in the royal palaces in and around Madrid. Ponz went on to lament the lack of reproductions without which they had remained unknown in Europe, adding that Spain now had plenty of competent engravers who could be put to work on such a project.

Ponz also printed in his guide the text of a letter by Anton Raffael Mengs concerning 'the most outstanding paintings preserved in the Royal Palace in Madrid'. This contained a description of the king's ante-chamber where most of the finest paintings by Spanish artists – Velasquez, Ribera and Murillo – were grouped together. Mengs praised Velasquez above all for the 'truth and knowledge of light and shade' in his pictures and for his understanding of the effect of aerial perspective in the relationship of near and distant objects. He went on to describe paintings from three different periods of Velasquez's career which hung in the great chamber – the early *Watercarrier of Seville*, the *Bacchus* and the *Forge of Vulcan*, and finally the late *Spinners*. He concluded that the study of these paintings would enable an artist to understand the path by which Velasquez had arrived 'at such excellence in the imitation of nature'.

Mengs at that time had an international reputation, and in inviting him to write his letter, Ponz was deliberately drawing attention to the great Spanish paintings in the royal collections as much as to the masterpieces of the other European schools. The proper appreciation of Spanish art had always been a subject of concern to the Academy of San Fernando whose Secretary Ponz had become in that same year. He found a powerful and enlightened supporter in the Count of Floridablanca who became Charles III's Secretary of State and as such Protector of the Academy in the following year; he and Ponz were apparently responsible for reviving a project already mooted in

7 *Aesop*, after Velasquez

8 *Baltasar Carlos*, after Velasquez

9 *Infante Don Fernando*, after Velasquez

10 *Las Meninas*, after Velasquez

11 *The blind guitarist*, after Goya's tapestry cartoon

1774 when the engraver Selma was to have been commissioned to reproduce paintings in the royal palaces.

With or without the active support of the Academy, Goya and two of his young colleagues took up the challenge and in 1778 were working on prints after Italian and Spanish seventeenth-century masters. Goya apparently reserved to himself the works of Velasquez and was the first to publish his prints. Ponz welcomed his initiative in a further volume of his guide published in July 1778, commending Goya for his 'capacity, intelligence and conscientious desire to serve the Nation, for which lovers of Velasquez and of painting must be grateful to him'. On the 28th of the same month, the *Gazeta de Madrid* carried an advertisement for 'Nine prints drawn and engraved in etching by Don Francisco Goya, Painter' after pictures by Velasquez, including five equestrian portraits, the figures of Menippus and Aesop and two dwarfs. It gave their prices (six reals for the equestrian portraits, three for the others) and the addresses of the two bookshops in Madrid where they could be purchased.

Eight of the prints were shown at the Academy and immediately justified the hopes of everyone concerned since they attracted the attention of a particularly distinguished foreigner, P. P. Giusti, the Viennese representative in Madrid. He wrote to the Austrian Grand Chancellor to inform him of the 'long-awaited start which a Spanish artist has made on the project for engraving the best paintings in the Royal Collections', commenting that the artist was a painter and not an engraver and was reproducing the paintings of Velasquez by the etching process. His letter accompanied a set of the prints and described it as making 'an important contribution to the world of the arts', which would particularly benefit 'other artists, who are almost entirely ignorant of the price-less treasures to be found in the Royal Palace at Madrid'.

In December, two further etchings were advertised and during the five intervening months Goya was apparently struggling with a novel development of the etching process, the new technique of aquatint, which might enable him, by adding tonal effects to his prints, to come closer to the painterly qualities of Velasquez's originals. However, of the six known prints with aquatint in the series after Velasquez, only two were apparently completed to Goya's satisfaction and given engraved titles. The others are known from a few proofs and were either abandoned or accidentally destroyed in the course of reworking the plates to achieve the effects Goya wanted. His interpretation of Velasquez's masterpiece, *Las Meninas*, is known in four or more states, the last of which (in Boston) has an added aquatint grain which spoils the effect of the composition. Goya may have lost still more plates, since there are four drawings which were certainly made for this series but of which no prints are known. One of them is a red chalk study (in Hamburg) of Velasquez's most famous early painting, the *Watercarrier of Seville* (now at Apsley House), which was described in Mengs's letter. The imprint of a copperplate on the paper shows that the drawing was transferred, although no etching is known. Goya must also have intended to reproduce paintings such as the *Forge of Vulcan* and the *Spinners* but abandoned the project, probably discouraged by the technical difficulties he encountered.

Goya made preparatory drawings for his prints in a variety of techniques: pen and ink, and black or red chalk. Only a very few drawings have survived but, unlike the pen and ink studies which he had used for his *San Francisco* and the *Garrotted man*, these are mainly in red chalk for the unpublished aquatinted plates. Ceán Bermúdez owned many of these preparatory drawings, of which the largest group is now in the Kunsthalle in Hamburg.

The characteristic freedom of Goya's approach is very well demonstrated in the

9 drawing and the five different states of the portrait of the *Infante Don Fernando* (of which
the British Museum proof, acquired in 1851, shows the state before the final aquatint).
In the delicate red chalk drawing, the composition is already markedly different from the
painting, the figure stockier and less elegant, the dog smaller, the landscape barely
indicated. Both here and in the early states in pure etching, Goya's understanding of
Velasquez's effects have led to a virtual suppression of all outlines, to a fine but vigorous
patterning of parallel lines which move round the forms, cutting off at the point where
the surface turns away out of sight. This conveys a vivid sense of solid forms surrounded
by air and atmosphere – the very qualities to which Mengs referred – while sharp zigzag
accents give vitality to the forms themselves.

   This drawing method was developed by Goya and is still recognisable in his extreme
96 old age, when his hand was shaky but remarkably sure, and when he is said to have
mocked the academicians and their methods, saying 'Always lines, and never any form.
But where do they find these lines in nature?'. Velasquez taught him to see in nature
'only forms that are lit up and forms that are not, planes which advance and planes which
recede, relief and depth'. This was the secret that enabled him to capture 'the magic of
the atmosphere of a picture', an expression which his son said that he always used.
Goya's copies after Velasquez prepared the ground for major developments in his art.
His painting became more fluent and atmospheric, and he acquired confidence and
greater subtlety and individuality in his drawing. This period of intense involvement
with printmaking was to bear fruit twenty years later in the first of his four great series
of prints, *Los Caprichos*.

3 The Caprichos

On 17 January 1799, Goya signed a receipt for 'four books of *caprichos* engraved by etching by my hand', which the Duke and Duchess of Osuna added to their already extensive collection of his works. Goya's 'collection of prints of "capricious" subjects' was announced in two Madrid newspapers, on 6 and 19 February. It was advertised for sale not in a bookshop, as was normal with prints, but in a shop selling perfume and spirits in the building in the Calle del Desengaño where Goya was living at that time. The edition appears to have been withdrawn from sale almost immediately, after threats of action by the Inquisition (to which Goya referred in his old age). Although the prints seem to have been known at least within a limited circle and to have had a certain *succès de scandale* at the time of their publication, Goya kept the bulk of the edition out of sight until he succeeded, either directly or through the intervention of Godoy, in negotiating the sale of the copperplates to Charles IV in 1803, when he handed them over to the Royal Chalcography together with 240 complete sets which had already been printed.

Los Caprichos, a series of eighty satirical prints, is generally regarded as Goya's first truly original work and its publication in 1799 has been seen as a symbolic watershed separating the eighteenth from the nineteenth centuries, the world of tapestry cartoons and decorative pictures and of a courtly type of portraiture from the powerful, imaginative works which made Goya's reputation as the forerunner of the Romantics and 'first of the moderns'. From the time his tapestry cartoons and etchings after Velasquez were favourably noticed in Madrid, Goya's career slowly gathered momentum. He painted altarpieces, decorative pictures and increasing numbers of portraits for institutions and aristocratic patrons, including the Dukes and Duchesses of Osuna and of Alba. As his fame grew, so did his independence of thought and judgement. In 1792 Goya delivered a report to the Academy of San Fernando concerning teaching methods and the Secretary of the Academy noted that 'Goya declared himself openly for freedom in teaching and stylistic practice'. His report contained a violent attack on neo-classical principles and the academic preference for an art based on study of the Greeks and the observance of 'good taste' rather than on direct observation of nature and the free expression of an artist's individual talent.

Reports on teaching in the Academy had been submitted by all the professors at the request of the newly-appointed Vice-Protector, Don Bernardo de Iriarte, an enlightened civil servant who was also a connoisseur and collector. Fifteen months later, in January 1794, after suffering the nearly fatal illness which left him permanently deaf, Goya wrote to Iriarte, sending him 'a set of cabinet pictures in which I have been able to make observations for which there is normally no opportunity in commissioned works which give no scope for *capricho* [fantasy] and invention . . .'. Three days later he wrote another letter – crucial for an understanding of his attitude to originality and imagination – in which he described in detail the picture he was painting to complete the set and which represented a scene that he had actually witnessed in a lunatic asylum in Saragossa. (Both letters are among the Egerton manuscripts in the British Museum.)

12 Announcement of the publication of the *Caprichos*

13 *They say yes and give their hand to the first comer* (Caprichos 2)

14 *Which of them is the more overcome?* (Caprichos Plate 27)

15 *Nobody knows himself* (Caprichos Plate 6)

Goya had fallen ill in Andalusia and had been looked after in Cadiz by Sebastián Martínez, a wealthy merchant who was a collector and a friend of Ceán Bermúdez. He owned hundreds of paintings and an extensive print collection, including etchings by Piranesi, which Goya would have been able to study during his convalescence. In 1796, two years after completing his little cabinet pictures, Goya went again to Andalusia and stayed with Ceán Bermúdez in Seville and then with the Duchess of Alba at Sanlúcar de Barrameda, following the death of her husband. On her country estate at Sanlúcar, Goya seems to have experienced an idyllic interlude suggested by the famous portrait, which he kept in his own collection (now Hispanic Society of America, New York), with its inscription *Solo Goya* in the sand at the Duchess's feet and their names inscribed on two rings on her fingers. The idyll may have ended in bitterness and deception, but while it lasted Goya filled a little album with enchanting, intimate brush and wash sketches of the capricious Duchess and her entourage. After her return to Madrid, he went to Cadiz where he remained until the following spring, having again fallen ill. A second sketchbook, almost certainly started in Cadiz, opens with much more pungent and witty scenes. Like his earlier tapestry cartoons, these recreate, but now in a free and totally informal way, the little comedies of Ramón de la Cruz. Taking up the notions of *capricho* and invention, first seen in the little paintings of 1794, these drawings recall the passage in Ramón de la Cruz's prologue to his works referring to the theatre: 'There is and has been no greater originality . . . than to copy what can be seen, that is, to portray people, their speech and actions, and their customs . . .'. Goya's observations, recreated and composed in the pages of his sketchbook, show prostitutes and flighty young girls, boisterous *majos* and elegant gallants promenading and flirting on the *paseo*, with a few indoor scenes in a boudoir or a salon. The sheets are numbered but untitled until, half way through the album, the style changes. The delicate, transparent qualities of the light-hearted brush and ink wash drawings give way to a harsher, bolder handling and the wit and humour turn to cruel, mordant satire. Terse titles explain or comment on the scenes, some of which are titled 'Masques' or 'Caricatures', and mocking, satirical scenes of witchcraft are followed by sometimes brutal allegories with erotic overtones, alluding to sexual perversion and excess, to moral and physical degeneracy and to anti-social behaviour at all levels of society.

It has been suggested that this sudden emergence of a satirical intention and a correspondingly dramatic graphic style was due to the influence of English caricatures, particularly those of Gillray, which are known to have interested the satirical writer, Leandro Fernández de Moratín. Moratín was close to Jovellanos and a leading figure of the Spanish Enlightenment. Protected by Godoy, he travelled extensively outside Spain, and in 1792 spent a year in London where he wrote a long note about the remarkable ferocity and effectiveness of the satirical caricatures which were published there in such numbers and in which 'all the vices of man in society are exposed to laughter and public scorn'. At the end of 1796, Moratín returned to Spain, spending his first few weeks in Cadiz where he is known to have had many meetings with Goya as well as their mutual friend, Sebastián Martínez. Political caricature, as Moratín noted, could be a weapon more powerful than the bitterest criticism or satire, and in England neither a king and his ministers nor the gravest judge or most learned author could escape being held up to ridicule. No such caricatures were allowed in Spain, although humorous and satirical prints for the Spanish market were published across the French border, in Bayonne. As he had responded to the need for reproductions of the masterpieces of Spanish art in 1778, so, on a quite different plane but still in the context of the Enlightenment, Goya responded to the need for a set of satirical prints which could parallel the writings of his liberal friends who were trying to reform the social and political life of the country.

By 1796, Spain was in a state of confusion. After the death of Charles III in 1789, his relatively stable regime of enlightened despotism quickly disintegrated. The outbreak of the French Revolution and the characters of Charles IV and María Luisa, the new monarchs, began to produce violent upheavals at court and in the country as a whole. The repercussions of the events in France, the execution of Louis XVI and the invasion of Spain's northern provinces provoked plots and counter-plots. The old king's minister of state, Floridablanca, reacted by trying to stem the tide of liberal thought and activity in Spain, but in 1792, as the queen's lover, Manuel Godoy, rose to high office, he was banished and Godoy took over the office of Secretary of State and with it the Protectorship of the Academy. Now in, now out of favour with the capricious and dissolute queen, Godoy was assailed alternately by the liberals and the ultra-conservatives. In 1795, more by good luck than good management, he emerged as Spain's saviour with the title 'Prince of the Peace' through the Treaty of Basle by which the French troops were withdrawn from Spain. The situation, however, soon deteriorated again and Godoy was attacked from all sides as the country reached the brink of financial ruin. The dissatisfaction of the liberals was expressed in a spate of critical and satirical poems and pamphlets, many of which, like the celebrated *Pan y Toros*, were circulated in manuscript form because of the severe censorship controls.

Goya, who had been appointed Court Painter on the accession of Charles IV and María Luisa, apparently felt secure enough to disregard the possible dangers to his position and standing at court and began turning his witty, satirical drawings into a set of caricatures which could be published and given a wide circulation. As with the copies after Velasquez, Goya must also have hoped that the venture would be a profitable one. The paintings which he sent to Iriarte in 1794 were made, according to his letter, partly in the hope of compensating for the expense of his recent illness. In April 1797 he gave up his post as Director of Painting at the Academy on the grounds of his continuing ill-health and was earning relatively little by his painting. Isolated to some extent by his deafness from normal social life, embittered by his encounter with the Duchess of Alba at Sanlúcar (although nothing is known for certain about their relationship), with wounding personal experiences of the rivalry of colleagues and the spectacle of immorality and intrigue at the court, Goya's view of society was ripe for expression in a wide range of satirical themes.

Numerous meetings with Moratín are recorded throughout the second half of 1797, the year in which Goya dated a drawing for a title page to his projected series of prints. A conspiracy against Godoy, who was in sympathy with the liberals, prompted the favourite to give them his full support, and in November Jovellanos was appointed Minister of Justice and Saavedra became Minister of Finance. The members of this progressive, liberal government were painted by Goya in a series of sympathetic portraits (that of Saavedra is in the Courtauld Institute Galleries) and Iriarte, whom he had recently portrayed in his capacity as Vice-Protector of the Academy, was also made a minister. The political climate appeared favourable and Goya continued with his project. However, in the spring of 1798, Godoy was forced to resign as Prime Minister and by August both Jovellanos and Saavedra (who had replaced him) were ousted from power and their places were taken respectively by Caballero and Urquijo, the one unscrupulous and ultra-conservative, and the other a professed radical of considerable cynicism and depravity, who first deputised for Saavedra and then replaced him as Minister of Finance and Foreign Affairs, and therefore also as Protector of the Academy, in February 1799, the month in which Goya's *Caprichos* were advertised for sale.

16 *Here comes the bogey-man* (*Caprichos* Plate 3)

Ni así la distingue.

17 *Even thus he cannot make her out* (*Caprichos* Plate 7)

Todos Caerán.

18 *All will fall* (*Caprichos* Plate 19)

Estan calientes.

19 *They are hot* (*Caprichos* Plate 13)

Que se la llevaron.

20 *They carried her off* (*Caprichos* Plate 8)

The *Caprichos* were issued as a paperbound album at a price of 320 reals for the set of
43 eighty prints. Only the rare presentation volumes, in contemporary leather bindings, have a title which appears on the spine: CAPRICHOS DE GOYA. There is no title-page or
1 printed explanation and the first print is the famous self-portrait of the artist in profile, his expression proud and sardonic, and with his name and occupation engraved in the lower margin. This is followed by a series of images which satirise the vices and follies of
13 contemporary Spanish society. After the sinister wedding of a masked and two-faced aristocratic young lady to an elderly gentleman – 'They say yes, and give their hand to
16 the first comer' – two prints refer to the bad upbringing of children, and the harmful
14–15, 17, 19 results are recorded in scenes illustrating the immorality and deceit practised by men and women who appear alternately as aggressors and victims. Goya explores the themes of superstition and sensuality, of greed and violence, with all their attendant ills. He shows smugglers turned to brigandry (a very serious evil in Andalusia), mocks dying
19, 21 lovers and carousing monks, and devotes many plates to prostitutes, at first pampered and predatory, then persecuted and imprisoned, while innocents are hounded by the
28 Inquisition. Titled idiots and quacks and the miserly and immoral clergy are held up to ridicule. Ignorance and stupidity are as savagely caricatured as immorality and the more flagrant vices, and the first part of the book is rounded off with the series of 'asses' – a traditional theme of the upside-down world – who play the parts of a teacher, a music
29–30 lover, a 'pure-bred' aristocrat, a doctor, a person of importance having his portrait painted by a monkey, and finally appear as the ignorant and 'beastly' oppressors of the poor.

At this point, a new chapter opens with a plate showing the artist asleep at a work-
31 table covered in papers and drawing instruments. On it appears the famous title *El sueño de la razon produce monstruos*, 'The sleep of reason engenders monsters'. Night creatures loom out of the darkness behind the sleeping figure and an owl offers him a crayon-holder. By this device, Goya implies that, unlike the caricatures of everyday life on the *paseo* or in the brothels and salons and prisons of Madrid in the first part of the album, the scenes which follow are fantastic images which have emerged from the realms of dream and nightmare. Witches and demons, spirits and phantoms now conceal and obscure the criticism in images which are, if anything, more violent in their satire than those in the first half of the volume. It is significant that more prints in which high-ranking
37, 39 personages have traditionally been identified – the Dowager Duchess of Osuna, Godoy and the Duchess of Alba – are included in this second section, and that Goya excluded from the album two related prints which he or his friends must have judged unsuitable for publication.

The idea of a set of satirical subjects germinated in the second, so-called Madrid Album of drawings already described. When Goya decided to make a set of prints for publication, a project which he must have discussed at length with Moratín, Ceán and other friends, he chose the age-old device of a series of *Sueños*, 'Dreams', which authors have so often used as a cover for their criticism of society. The *Sueño* drawings were made in pen and brown ink and were transferred to the copperplates in the usual way, ink wash being added at a later stage as a guide for aquatint. The *Sueño 1°*, 'First Dream', which
31 later became the half-way chapter heading as Plate 43 of the *Caprichos*, has two inscriptions: on the table is the title of the work, 'Universal language. Drawn and Engraved by Francisco de Goya in the year 1797', and below the design is a longer subtitle, 'The Author dreaming. His only intention is to banish harmful common beliefs and to perpetuate with this work of *caprichos* the sound testimony of truth'. There follow, in the 'Dream' drawing sequence, ten scenes of witchcraft, devoted to the

21 *She prays for her* (*Caprichos* Plate 31). Proof before burnishing of aquatint, for example in the girl's arm and skirt, and extensive burin work in her hair, and with manuscript title

22–4 Details of 21, of a first edition impression showing burnishing of aquatint and addition of touches of drypoint to girl's bodice, and of a fourth edition impression showing the wear of the aquatint grain and the extent of the burin rework in the hair

25 *And his house is on fire* (Caprichos Plate 18)

26 *Because she was susceptible* (Caprichos Plate 32)

education and training of novice witches and the remarkable habits and customs of their seniors. However, in the '11th Dream', Goya turned to visions more directly applicable to contemporary Spanish society. A particularly obscene subject showing a hermaphrodite is concerned with ideas of deceit and sexual depravity and appeared as one of the earliest 'Masques' in the Madrid Album; it was reworked in another, much less explicit 38 drawing before being etched as Plate 57 of the *Caprichos*. Many of the *Sueño* drawings elaborate and transform sketches and ideas in the Madrid Album: it provides the source 33 for two of the witchcraft scenes, as well as for the brigands, the carousing monks and the 'Literary Ass' which appear among the later 'Dream' drawings and are included as prints 19 in the first part of the *Caprichos* (Plates 11, 13 and 39).

When Goya took the decision to make a much more extensive series of prints, he began to work in red chalk, as he had in most of the copies after Velasquez. The pen and ink of the *Sueño* drawings is closer to the effect of etching but may thereby have given too precise an image when transferred to the copperplate, leaving the artist less scope for the free play of his etching needle. One of the red chalk drawings appears on the back of a preliminary pen and ink study for the '1st Dream', in which a copperplate leaning against the artist's chair has been identified as of one of the equestrian portraits after Velasquez. The red chalk drawing on the verso was made for one of the later etchings 15 placed near the front of the *Caprichos* album (Plate 6). Less overtly erotic than the drawing, where the noses and tall hats are more exaggerated, the print entitled *Nadie se conoce*, 'No one knows himself', shows Goya's style at its most expressive, his superb draughtsmanship complemented by a bold and brilliant use of aquatint with softly burnished half-tones and dramatic highlights. The earlier prints, made from the *Sueño* drawings, are characterised by lighter, less insistent etching and by a simpler use of pale 14, 32–3 tones of aquatint (Plates 27, 68 and 70).

In the 1790s, printmakers in Spain were still using the aquatint technique in a rather limited way for decorative, historical and topographical subjects. Goya probably saw French and perhaps English prints which used a variety of aquatint effects, but an intriguingly close parallel with the *Caprichos* prints is to be found in a set of genre subjects etched, aquatinted and published by Giovanni David of Genoa in Venice in 1775. In these, not only the free, painterly handling of the aquatint but also the scale and style of the compositions suggest a possible direct influence (which again raises the question of Goya's contacts with Domenico Tiepolo who had acquired a copy of the *Caprichos* by the time of his death in Venice in 1804). Goya's handling of the aquatint medium is, however, very far from David's urbane and decorative style; he developed the dramatic contrast of light and shade, through the biting and burnishing of richly textured or velvet-smooth aquatint grains, to express opposing forces of enlightenment and ignorance, of reason and the irrational world, and to suggest an atmosphere of violence and doom. He became so expert in the handling of aquatint that in the famous 21 print of the old *celestina* praying over a prostitute, he changed the entire effect of the design by removing large areas of tone and then reworking the plate with a new aquatint 22–4 and with drypoint and burin. The proof before the rework (acquired by the British Museum from the Burty collection in 1876) contrasts strikingly with the final state in the edition of 1799, while a later impression shows up the extent of the burin rework in the 26 girl's hair. Goya's virtuosity is demonstrated in two pure aquatint prints (Plates 32 and 39), in which no etched lines or even burnishing are used.

The development of Goya's designs can be followed very closely, from the light-hearted sketches in the early albums to the most powerfully dramatic of the later prints. The development of his ideas is seen in the brief titles or longer inscriptions which he

27 *Hush* (*Caprichos* Plate 28)

28 *Why hide them?* (*Caprichos* Plate 30)

29 *Neither more nor less* (*Caprichos* Plate 41)

30 *Thou who canst not* (*Caprichos* Plate 42)

El sueño de la razon produce monstruos

31 *The sleep of reason produces monsters* (*Caprichos* Plate 43)

32 *Pretty teacher!* (*Caprichos* Plate 68)

33 *Devout profession* (*Caprichos* Plate 70)

34 *Tale-bearers* or *Blasts of wind* (*Caprichos* Plate 48)

35 *A gift for the master* (*Caprichos* Plate 47)

added to many of the drawings and proofs of the prints before deciding on the title to be engraved on the copperplate. In the Madrid Album, the titles sometimes take the form of exclamatory comments and sometimes provide longer, ironic descriptions of the scenes, as do those on the later *Sueño* drawings and some of the working proofs of the prints. The final titles on the prints are generally short and less explicit. They must have been engraved on the copperplates when the whole series had been completed and put in order, prior to the printing of the edition during the winter of 1798. By this time, the liberals had already fallen from power and Goya was bound to take precautions to conceal the extent of his satire. The text of the announcement which was published in the *Diario de Madrid* in February 1799, and which may have been drafted by Moratín, emphasises the general nature of Goya's caricature and states that 'in none of the compositions . . . has the artist intended to ridicule the particular defects of any one individual'. A manuscript attributed to Goya, and which may also have been composed by Moratín, provides bland and generalised explanations of each of the eighty plates. This manuscript (now in the Prado) was copied and widely circulated, but other manuscripts record interpretations of the prints by contemporaries in which individual figures are identified as the queen, Godoy, the Duchess of Alba and, in Plate 32, the 26 unfaithful 'wife of Castillo' whose trial and execution for aiding and abetting the murder of her husband created a sensation in Madrid in 1797 and 1798. References to the Inquisition are also pointed out, as well as to monks and nuns whose identity Goya obscured, often by showing them as goblins or witches.

Whether or not all these particular identifications are valid, the *Caprichos* constitute a unique, illustrated exposé of some of the 'follies and errors', the 'common prejudices and lies' which afflicted Spanish society at the end of the eighteenth century, and the prints express, in vivid visual form, the ideas and interests and sometimes dangerously critical views of Goya's enlightened, liberal friends. A copy of the draft announcement for the *Diario de Madrid*, which is found in the set of the *Caprichos* which Goya gave to his friend 43 Ceán Bermúdez (now in the Harris collection in the British Museum), shows that Goya intended not only to announce a subscription for the *Caprichos* but also to sell the work through a bookseller, in the normal way. He changed his mind, dropped the idea of a 12 subscription (which could have compromised those whose names would appear on the list) and put the prints on sale himself in a shop which had nothing to do with prints and books but was conveniently situated next to his home. Thirteen days elapsed between the first announcement in the *Diario* and the second, abbreviated one, which appeared in the *Gazeta de Madrid* on 19 February, between advertisements for a new map of Estremadura and books of music, including choral works by Haydn and Pergolesi. The prints were then withdrawn (Goya later stated that they had been on sale for only two days) and it may have been at this time that the generalised explanations of the Prado manuscript were written, to answer any criticism from the Inquisition or from government circles.

Very few contemporary reactions to the *Caprichos* are recorded and neither Moratín nor Jovellanos are known to have referred to them directly. The earliest critical reference, recently published, is a remark by the court engraver Pedro González de Sepúlveda, a friend of Goya, Jovellanos and Ceán, who noted in his diary between 14 and 21 February 1799, immediately after the advertisement of the *Caprichos* in the *Diario de Madrid*, that he had seen at the home of Pedro de Arnal, a fellow academician and the Duchess of Alba's architect, 'the book of witches and satires by Goya, I didn't like it, it is very licentious'. Other comments suggest that the *Caprichos* were seen as hilarious or witty caricature. Two serious critical appreciations, both published in Cadiz in 1811 (by

Tragata perro.

36 *Swallow it, dog* (*Caprichos* Plate 58)

37 *To rise and to fall* (Caprichos Plate 56)

38 *The filiation* (Caprichos Plate 57)

39 *Until death* (Caprichos Plate 55)

40 *What a golden beak!* (Caprichos Plate 53)

Gregorio González Azaola in the *Semanario Patriótico* and by Antonio Puigblanch in a pseudonymous book on the Inquisition), refer to the artist's more serious, satirical intentions, and Azaola pointed out that although the average person took them to be absurd extravaganzas of their author, more perceptive people realised that each contained some enigmatic meaning, adding that their subtlety was such that even the sharpest minds did not grasp the full moral meaning of some of them at first sight.

The insight this critical view affords into contemporary understanding of the *Caprichos* prints underlines the complexity of Goya's 'Universal language'. His circle of intellectual friends and colleagues must have recognised many of the literary references in the prints, beginning with the quotation from a satirical poem by Jovellanos in the title of Plate 2. Many scenes in the prints parallel passages in the satirical writings of Padre Isla on a ridiculous preaching friar, and of Feijóo on the subject of witches and goblins, of Samaniego the fabulist, and of Moratín the poet and playwright, besides earlier sources in Quevedo's critical 'Dreams', and the many neo-classical versions of the Horatian concept of monsters of imagination created by the dreams of sick and delirious men, of which Goya's 'Sleep of reason' is an obvious paraphrase. References to contemporary plays have been identified, for example in the satire on the nobility in Plate 50. Two of the witchcraft scenes which Goya painted in 1797–8 for the Duke and Duchess of Osuna, including the one in the National Gallery in London, were directly based on scenes from plays by Antonio de Zamora. The subject of witchcraft itself was enormously popular both with the common people and with intellectuals like Moratín who wrote his witty, satirical commentary on the celebrated account of the *Auto da fé . . . in Logroño . . . in 1610* during the period when Goya was working on the drawings which were to evolve into the *Caprichos* prints. The ludicrous, gruesome or obscene events described in the course of the witches' trial are paralleled in many of Goya's witchcraft scenes, and their explanations in the so-called Prado commentary are remarkably close to many of Moratín's annotations to the *Auto da fé*.

Nothing is known of Goya's specific literary interests, since the inventory of his home made in 1812 does not list the books in his library. It is worth noting that the library of his brother-in-law, Francisco Bayeu, included the fables of Samaniego, *Don Quixote*, the collected works of Quevedo and Padre Isla's satirical writings, and it is reasonable to suppose that Goya owned a wide selection of books, including those which his literary friends must have given him. He had access to many libraries – in the Academy, at the houses of his aristocratic patrons and of his friends and colleagues – where he could consult not only the Spanish classics but also collections of foreign books, in the original or in translation. In particular, French illustrated books, both moralising and licentious, with their engraved frontispieces and illustrations, provided a rich source of inspiration.

Goya's autograph captions on his prints and drawings and the expressive phrases for his letters to friends show a lively enjoyment of language and are often admirable in their brevity and sardonic wit. Goya's own style was earthy rather than elegant and he used and evidently appreciated the directness and evocative richness of popular speech – proverbial expressions, tags and catchphrases, the punning language of the lower classes which could so effectively be expressed in the interplay of word and image in the prints and their titles. The titles of Plates 23 and 42 are parts of well-known proverbs; Plates 19, 20, 21 and 35, which refer to the activities of prostitutes, play on the meanings of *desplumar*, 'to pluck', and *descañonar*, 'to shave', both meaning to 'fleece' or 'rob', while Plates 45, 48 and 69 make use of the multiple meanings of *chupar*, 'to suck' or 'swindle', and *soplar*, 'to blow', 'have a blow-out' or 'split on', with reference to the habits of witches or of monks and nuns thinly disguised as witches. In other cases, the

71.

Si amanece ; nos Vamos.

41 *When day breaks we will be off* (Caprichos Plate 71)

image alone refers to a figure of speech: *hacer capa*, 'to cloak' or 'shield', is enacted literally in Plate 21 where a magistrate covers up for two cat-constables devouring a hen-prostitute, and metaphorically in Plates 51 and 69 where winged demons hide the evil doings of their colleagues.

These visual images are brilliant inventions of the artist, but others derive from age-old traditional imagery. The most striking example is the sequence of 'asses', already mentioned, possibly derived from the near-contemporary set of caricatures published in Bayonne in 1792 but which goes back ultimately, as do the Bayonne prints, to the ancient imagery of the 'world upside-down' or 'topsy-turvy world', in which the divine order and the world of rational, reasonable man are upset and inverted by the passions of man's lower nature. The themes are comic but there are strong moralising overtones: the ass as teacher and doctor, a monkey playing a guitar to an ass, and the archetypal upside-down image of asses riding on men. Even the image in Plate 26, where a pun on the word *asiento*, meaning both 'chair' and 'sense', is illustrated by obviously scatter-brained girls with chairs on their heads, is a traditional topsy-turvy image where the chair sits on the person.

Another source of imagery on which Goya drew throughout his career is that contained in books of emblems – allegorical images which were used to express all manner of philosophical and moral ideas. The best known are the *Emblemata* of Alciati and the *Iconologia* of Ripa, published in the 1530s and 1590s respectively, but many emblem books and 'Iconographies' were published or reprinted in the seventeenth and eighteenth centuries and Goya probably owned a number of such works. In Plate 19, the allegory of the bird-woman decoy in the tree, surrounded by bird-men lovers, of whom the engraved caption says simply 'All will fall' as they drop down to be plucked (or 'fleeced') by the women waiting below, is based on a traditional satirical image of love. A number of other plates have been related to emblematic imagery and it is significant that in the French *Iconographie* of Gravelot and Cochin published in 1791 which Goya certainly knew and used, the introductory text refers to emblematic allegory as a *langue universelle*, the 'universal language' of the title-page to Goya's *Sueños*.

The language of the *Caprichos* is an extraordinarily rich and subtle one. The title itself evokes the *Vari capricci* and other imaginative etchings of Giambattista Tiepolo, and artistic as well as literary and iconographical sources can be recognised in these prints. But more significant than particular parallels with Tiepolo or Fragonard, with contemporary French engravings or the aquatints of Le Prince or Giovanni David, is the profound influence of Rembrandt in Goya's work at this period and throughout his later career. His sketches for a number of religious works and the large painting of the *Taking of Christ* executed in 1798 have strong Rembrandtesque qualities and the latter picture is remarkably similar to one of the most disturbing prints in the *Caprichos*, which shows a man mocked and threatened, in this case by members of the Church (Plate 58). Ceán recorded that he gave a number of Rembrandt prints to Goya while he was working on the *Caprichos*, and Goya himself is known to have had ten in his own collection by 1812. After his study of Velasquez in 1778, his interest in Rembrandt twenty years later was to have a decisive influence on his ability to create emotion and generate dramatic tension in his prints by the most direct means, creating powerfully natural effects in individual figures and in their relationship to each other within a simple, luminous composition or one shrouded in richly evocative darkness.

42 Drawing of the Duke of Wellington

4 The Disasters of War

In spite of the publication of his satirical *Caprichos* early in 1799, by the autumn Goya was working on a series of royal portraits, which culminated in the great *Family of Charles IV* completed in 1801. He was appointed First Court Painter and was in close touch with Godoy, whose enchanting, pregnant wife he also painted. In the same year, Godoy acquired Goya's house in the Calle del Desengaño for his mistress, Pepita Tudo, the celebrated actress. In the following year Goya made a flamboyant portrait of Godoy himself, the all-powerful 'Prince of the Peace' who was by now supporting the reactionary clerical party. In 1801, Jovellanos was imprisoned, Ceán Bermúdez went to Seville and many of Goya's liberal, intellectual friends were persecuted. The Duchess of Alba died in mysterious circumstances in 1802, leaving a pension to Goya's son. Goya's position must have been made more insecure by the replacement, at the end of that year, of Iriarte as Vice-Protector of the Academy (later, in 1804, he was disgraced and exiled).

In July 1803 Goya wrote to the minister Miguel Cayetano Soler to confirm (as though the idea had been suggested by someone else – possibly Godoy) that he wished to offer the eighty copperplates of the *Caprichos* as a gift to the king, adding that this was for fear that after his death they might fall into the hands of the foreigners who showed so much interest in them. An annual pension for his son was all he asked in exchange and this was granted in order that 'Don Francisco Xavier should travel to foreign countries and, by instructing himself in painting, should distinguish himself like his maternal grandfather [presumably his uncle Francisco Bayeu] and his father', a project which he seems never to have fulfilled.

After 1803, during the period of reactionary government, Goya seems to have had no direct contact with the court although he continued to draw his salary as Court Painter. His portraits included more professional and middle-class people and he painted and drew for his own pleasure, taking up again the practice of making albums of drawings in which he recorded his private thoughts and fantasies. During these years of relative calm, Napoleon was carrying out his conquest of Europe, while Godoy mismanaged the affairs of the country and the war against England (to which Spain was bound by the treaties signed with France). Both he and Ferdinand, the heir to the throne, were carrying on intrigues with Napoleon to secure their positions against each other. Napoleon finally determined to oust the Bourbons and replace them with a Bonaparte dynasty and early in 1808 his troops entered northern Spain. By this time, popular sympathy was entirely in favour of Ferdinand. After an intrigue caused his arrest on suspicion of treason, a violent uprising against Godoy forced Charles IV to dismiss the favourite and abdicate in favour of his son. Napoleon, however, summoned the entire royal family to Bayonne where they immediately capitulated to his demands. A new Constitution was prepared and Joseph Bonaparte was proclaimed king of Spain in June.

Meanwhile, on 2 May, when the youngest Infante was preparing to leave the palace in Madrid to join the Royal Family already in Bayonne, the loyal citizens, having no idea what was going on in France and being thoroughly alarmed for the safety of the Royal

44 Title-page of the Ceán album of the *Disasters of War*

45 Two proofs of *Prisoners* mounted at the end of the Ceán *Disasters* album

43 The three Ceán Bermúdez albums: *Caprichos*, *Disasters* and *Tauromaquia*

Family, began a riot in Madrid which grew to a pitched battle with Murat's troops. The bloody events of the 'Dos de mayo' were followed the next day by mass executions in reprisal, scenes immortalised by Goya in his two great paintings started in 1814 after the end of the war. As the news spread, the provinces rose one by one against the French and *44* 'the bloody war in Spain with Bonaparte' (as Goya called it) had begun. It was to last six long years, as the regular French troops (which included Poles and Mamelukes) found themselves blocked by the heroic resistance of cities like Saragossa, harassed by tenacious and well-organised guerrilla bands and confounded by the savage resistance of the civilian population, led by fanatical priests and friars in what became a crusade to restore the *deseado*, the 'desired' Ferdinand, and to expel Joseph Bonaparte and the French from Spain.

Goya was caught up in the events of the year 1808 but managed to live through the period of the war without declaring himself openly for or against the French. Many of his close friends such as Moratín, Iriarte, Meléndez Valdés and the actor Maíquez were *afrancesados* and supported Napoleon and his brother in the belief that Spain's institutions, both church and state, were so archaic and so profoundly corrupted that reform and constitutional government could only be imposed through French intervention. The choices to be made were far from clear, since those liberals who supported the anti-French national government found themselves in the same camp as the 'Serviles', the most reactionary proponents of absolute monarchy and the supremacy of the Church, whose fervent desire was the abolition of any form of constitutional government. Goya kept his opinions to himself, confiding them to his 'journal-albums' of drawings, and walked a political and moral tight-rope in order to ensure the security of his family and his way of life which seems to have been a comfortable one, at least until 1812. But there is ample proof of his emotional involvement in the course of the war and of his intense response to the sufferings of his country. He did not draw his salary as Court Painter during the French occupation, and is said to have shown his hatred of the French invaders, even leaving Madrid at one stage in an attempt to make his way to 'a free country'. Nevertheless, during these years Goya painted official portraits of Spain's rulers and of Spanish, French and English officials and officers in both the progressive and reactionary and the pro- and anti-Napoleon camps: Ferdinand VII in 1808 and again in 1814, Joseph Bonaparte in 1810 (in an allegorical painting whose subsequent alterations reflected the rapid changes of the political scene), Llorente and Romero, *afrancesados* who held important posts under Joseph, Palafox the patriotic Spanish general, as well as the French general Guye and the Duke of Wellington.

Two drawings and three paintings of the Iron Duke exist, commemorating his victory over the French at the Battle of Salamanca and his triumphal entry into Madrid *42* on 12 August 1812. The famous portrait drawing in the British Museum was acquired in 1862, with a note by Goya's grandson Mariano describing it as 'A drawing made at Alba de Tormes after the battle of Arapiles [Salamanca] of the Duke of Weelingthon [*sic*] as a study for the portrait'. The portrait in question was undoubtedly the large equestrian painting (now at Apsley House) which was executed at great speed and exhibited at the Academy during the first two weeks in September. The drawing is also related to the lively bust portrait in oils in the National Gallery, London, for which Wellington is said to have sat to Goya in Madrid. It shows an early stage of this painting, before alterations to the Duke's dress and additional decorations. The drawing is in red chalk and the paper shows traces of folds similar to those on many drawings which were transferred to a copperplate for etching (for example, the *Sueños* drawings, where the large sheets of paper were wrapped round the edges of the plate, causing a double foldline). That Goya's intention may well have been to make an etched portrait of the Duke is further suggested by the blank space between the lower edges of the design and the copperplate, which would have been engraved with a suitable inscription, as in the self-portrait of 1798.

1

In 1808 Goya was living in a house on the Calle de Valverde, in the next block to his old home where the *Caprichos* had been put on sale. His son Xavier was living just off the Puerta del Sol and Goya may even have witnessed the terrible fighting there on 2 May. In March, after the abdication of Charles IV and only four days after Ferdinand's arrival in Madrid, the Academy of San Fernando had commissioned Goya to paint a portrait of the new monarch. Its execution was delayed by the chaotic events that followed: the Spanish royal family's departure for Bayonne, the general uprising against the French, the arrival in Madrid of Joseph Bonaparte, and the Spanish victories which led to his flight. The first siege of Saragossa, brilliantly defended by Palafox, was lifted in August. In the following month a national government was formed under Floridablanca and Jovellanos. Goya probably did not start work on his portrait of Ferdinand for the Academy until this time, since he wrote on 2 October to inform the Secretary that it would be delivered and hung as soon as it was dry, but that he himself could not attend to this since he had been called by Palafox 'to go this week to Saragossa, to see and study the ruins of the city, in order to paint the glorious deeds of her citizens, a request which I cannot refuse since the honour and glory of my homeland are so close to my heart'. A few days later, Goya is recorded as having donated twenty-one yards of linen to the army of Aragon, his native province.

Goya was sixty-two when he set out, through the war-torn countryside, on the journey to Saragossa. He is said to have arrived there at the end of October and to have made sketches recording the events of the siege and the destruction of the city. Napoleon, however, entered Spain early in November and as the French troops closed in again on Saragossa, Goya apparently withdrew to the safety of his birthplace, the village of Fuendetodos. The works he executed at this time have not survived, but he must have seen enough on his journeys to and from Saragossa and in the city itself to provide material for many of his later works.

By the end of 1809 the last regular troops of the Spanish army had been routed, the British had retreated to Portugal and Napoleon's troops invaded Andalusia, driving the national government from Seville to Cadiz, where reactionary and democratic national-ists confronted each other as they faced the French from the last bastion of resistance. In the spring of 1810, the people of Spain turned on the French in a renewed and desperate onslaught of guerrilla warfare. The country was reduced to a state of ruin, fields were untended, villages ransacked and burned, and terrible atrocities were committed on both sides. It was in this year when Napoleon's troops had overrun almost the whole of Spain that Goya took up his etching tools once again and began work on a series of prints illustrating not the battles and major encounters of the war, not the ruins of Saragossa, but the anonymous incidents, the confused, isolated and violent events experienced by the ordinary people of Spain in their struggle against the French and against their own traitors, the *Josefinos*.

Neither Goya nor anyone close to him has left any recorded explanation of what his intentions were, and indeed they must have changed as the situation changed in Spain. He worked on the prints over a period of some ten years (1810–20) but was never able to publish them. Of the two complete sets of proofs which Goya is known to have put together, only the one which he gave to Ceán Bermúdez (now in the British Museum) was completed, with numbers and manuscript titles that remain the artist's only

46   *Charity* (*Disasters* Plate 27)

47   *I saw it* (*Disasters* Plate 44)

48 *And there's no help for it* (*Disasters* Plate 15)

49 *Ravages of war* (*Disasters* Plate 30)

43 written record for the series. The leather-bound volume, labelled (like the earlier series) CAPRICHOS DE GOYA on the spine, has a manuscript title-page, carefully lettered in ink

44 as a model for engraving, which was probably also composed by Goya and reads: 'Fatal consequences of the bloody war in Spain with Bonaparte. And other allegorical *caprichos*, in 85 prints. Invented, drawn and engraved by the original painter D. Francisco de Goya y Lucientes. In Madrid.' Below is a note by Valentín Carderera (see p. 99) stating that the manuscript titles are in Goya's own hand. The eighty-five prints are made up of

46–53 some forty-five plates devoted to the war and sixteen plates which record the terrible

54–6 year of famine in Madrid in 1811–12. The other twenty plates, including the 'allegorical

58–61 *caprichos*' of the title-page, a few additional plates inserted among the war and famine scenes as well as the frontispiece were probably added after 1814. Goya completed the

45 volume by pasting proofs of three little plates of *Prisoners* on to the last two pages. The *Prisoners*, probably etched about 1811, have manuscript titles referring to the barbarity of imprisonment and torture and they have been related to the debates of the Cortes in Cadiz concerning the abolition of torture which was proposed in that year and incorporated into the Cadiz Constitution of 1812.

The Ceán Bermúdez album, which is even signed by Goya on the closed sheet edges, is uniquely important not only because of the manuscript title-page, the autograph titles on the prints and the extra plates included in the volume, but also because it shows the series as Goya must have intended to publish it, and the way in which he intended the plates to be printed. The final suppression of liberalism and constitutional government in Spain in 1823, which led to Goya's decision to leave the country, prevented its publication. The copperplates remained in Madrid and eighty of them were eventually acquired by the Academy of San Fernando in 1862. The final two plates of the series were separated and never incorporated in any of the published editions. The collector Valentín Carderera, to whom Ceán's daughter had given the precious volume, lent it to the Academy so that the titles could be engraved on the plates for the first edition of the series which was published in 1863. This was done with great care, following the form of Goya's lettering and even copying several mistakes in spelling, punctuation and the use of capital and lower case letters (these mistakes were corrected during the printing of the edition). The Academy, however, unfortunately also saw fit to

57 make a number of alterations, in one case changing a title (Plate 69), in another adding

50 aquatint to a scratched and, in its eyes, defective plate (Plate 7). Most disastrous of all was the printing of the edition in 1863 not in accordance with the evidence of the sparkling and cleanly wiped proofs of the Ceán album, but to conform with the mid-nineteenth-century taste for impressions with a great deal of ink left on the surface of the plate in the wiping to give a rich overall tone, which quite transforms the effect of the images. The luminosity and delicacy of the impressions in the Ceán album (as in the large numbers of other proofs which Goya made) were completely lost in all the posthumous editions which only provide a dulled and distorted reflection of the artist's intentions.

As with all his other prints, Goya made preparatory drawings, mostly in red chalk, for the *Disasters of War*. Both drawings and prints have been shown to fall into distinctive groups which afford a fairly coherent understanding of the development of the series. Goya also gave (not infallible) indications of his first intentions by numbering many of the war and famine scenes in the lower left corner of the plates, before renumbering them when he put the entire series of eighty-two plates into its final order. The earliest etchings were almost always signed in the plate by Goya and they include most of the plates in the early sequence up to number 27. Among them are the three plates dated

46 1810 which have the earlier numbers 7, 8 and 11 (Plates 20, 22 and 27 of the final numbering). Almost all are scenes which Goya could have witnessed on his journeys to

47 and from Saragossa and one of the prints, inscribed *Yo lo vi*, 'I saw this', with the earlier number 15, shows refugees fleeing in panic through the countryside (Plate 44). The dated plates show desperately wounded Spanish soldiers being given first aid in the field, the corpses of armed civilians lying in piles on the bare ground, and the naked bodies of

46 dead men being thrown into a pit, under the gaze of an enigmatic onlooker who has sometimes been identified as Goya himself. The title of this print, *Caridad*, 'Charity', is typical of the terse, ironic comments and exclamations which Goya used to underline these horrifying or pathetic scenes.

48–9 Four particularly dramatic prints, numbered 20 to 23 according to the earlier sequence, throw light on Goya's working methods in the difficult period of the war. Whereas the prints up to the earlier number 19 are on plates of more or less uniform size, and it has been shown that their preparatory drawings are all on good quality Netherlandish paper, Goya clearly began to experience difficulty as imports ceased and stocks of paper and copperplates dwindled. Copperplates may even have become unobtainable for a while and Goya took the drastic step of destroying two beautiful

100 landscape plates, from which very few impressions had been printed, by cutting them in halves and using the backs for four war scenes: the rape of a woman by French soldiers in

49 front of her husband, an explosion inside a house, with its occupants hurtling to the

48 ground, the hanging of collaborators, and the execution by French firing squads of Spanish guerrillas in a scene which prefigures the great painting of the *Executions of the third of May*. Two of the preparatory drawings for these prints are even executed on the front and back of the same scrap of paper.

None of the war scenes is in any real sense an illustration of a particular event and only two have been definitely linked to known incidents. The first alludes to the heroic

50 act of Agustina, the 'maid of Saragossa', who in July 1808, during the first siege of the city, seized a match from a dying gunner and fired a cannon at the French when all who manned the battery had fallen. Although Goya does not name the girl (whom he probably met on his visit to Saragossa), the simple, dramatic representation and the title *Que valor!*, 'What courage!', would instantly have conveyed the print's significance to a contemporary audience (Plate 7). Agustina's deed, which was depicted in popular prints and re-enacted in the innumerable patriotic plays which were performed in Madrid whenever the city was free from French occupation, achieved international renown, seen for example in Wilkie's painting of 1828 now in the Royal Collection.

Goya's print of Agustina appears, like a number of others in the *Disasters* series, to have been based on the large aquatints depicting the ruins of Saragossa by his fellow-academicians Juan Galvez and Fernando Brambila who were in Saragossa at the same time as Goya. They subsequently worked on their copperplates in Madrid before re-treating from the occupying forces to Seville and finally to Cadiz where their prints were published in 1812. Although Goya may have seen them at work in Saragossa or Madrid, it is more probable that he did not know these prints until they reached Madrid after the siege of Cadiz was raised and Wellington's victories had forced the French from Madrid. If this is so, it provides a possible date for Goya's print of Agustina which fits its position as number 41 in the 'early' sequence, among the later war and famine scenes. It also supports the possibility that other prints were inspired by these aquatints since Goya's 'early' number 38 (Plate 64) may reflect a detail from one of Galvez and Brambila's complex and detailed scenes. Goya's shows a dead girl being loaded into a cart and he

54–6 placed it, in the final sequence, among the seventeen famine scenes which record with pathos and bitter cynicism the terrible fate of the inhabitants of Madrid, of whom 20,000 died of starvation in the year from August 1811 to 1812. At the same time, and on the same batch of copperplates, Goya added scenes of terrifying atrocities to his record of the war (Plates 31–9). One of them, showing a naked corpse impaled on a tree, is identified by an inscription on a working proof, as having occurred at Chinchón, where his younger brother Camilo had been a priest since 1783 and for whose parish church Goya painted an altarpiece which was apparently placed in position in June 1812.

The war and famine scenes were probably completed and numbered during the months between Wellington's entry into Madrid in August 1812 and the overthrow of the Constitution of Cadiz by Ferdinand VII in the spring of 1814. The early number sequence shows how Goya began, as he did all his series of prints, with lightly etched and aquatinted scenes in which many figures are placed in an often quite detailed setting. Later the figures are reduced in number and move forward to fill the foreground. The handling becomes bold and even rough in its use of direct washes of acid (lavis), coarsely granulated aquatint burnished to produce painterly, almost impasted effects, and a strong, deeply bitten etched line of extraordinary expressiveness. In the later war and famine scenes, the figures are sometimes combined in superbly balanced compositions with a tree or the outline of a building, and sometimes set against an abstract background of rich, grainy aquatint, recalling the most striking of the *Caprichos* plates. However, the comparison serves to show how firmly rooted the latter are in a fundamentally eighteenth-century pictorial style and how uncompromisingly 'modern' Goya's vision had become by the second decade of the nineteenth century.

Goya's recreation of fragments of a reality which he either saw himself or experienced in imagination through the accounts and depictions of others led to the creation of images which are timeless in their condemnation of the brutality of war and man's inhumanity to man. Once again, as in the case of the *Caprichos*, the key does not lie in contemporary caricature or illustration, in Gillray and Gamelin, Galvez and Brambila, or even Flaxman, although the influence of all of these has been demonstrated; it does not lie even in Callot's often-cited *Grandes Misères de la guerre*, which are so utterly unlike Goya's prints in style and approach. A more significant parallel is found in the rich humanity, the pathos and emotion, the strength and even violence of Rembrandt's prints which appear to have played a crucial role in Goya's presentation of his theme. His scenes of confusion and struggle, of panicked civilians and fleeing refugees, recall the welter and scattering of men and animals in Rembrandt's *Christ driving the moneychangers from the Temple* and above all in the *Angel appearing to the shepherds*, which has always been compared with the painting of the *Colossus*. The handling of some of the war scenes suggests parallels with the *Stoning of St Stephen* and the *Sacrifice of Isaac*, while the famine scenes, with their dark aquatint backgrounds or framing arches and pillars, evoke Rembrandt's *Peter and John with the lame beggar*. In Plate 55 of the *Disasters*, a comely young Spanish girl passing beside a group of skeletal, starving figures on her way to meet a handsome French soldier is a modern paraphrase of the traditional theme of Death and the maiden, which also appears in a rare etching by Rembrandt, paralleled more closely still in Goya's preparatory drawing where a young man and the girl walk arm in arm. This print is one of several where well-to-do bourgeois citizens are contrasted with the pathetic poor.

The series, as finally numbered by Goya, opens with a plate showing a kneeling figure with arms outstretched, his pose and expression recalling traditional representations of Christ's agony in the garden (the subject of a celebrated little picture traditionally attributed to Goya). The print introduces the series with the title 'Sad

7

Que Valor!

50 *What courage!* (*Disasters* Plate 7)

4

Las mugeres dan valor

51 *The women give courage* (*Disasters* Plate 4)

Grande hazaña con muertos

52 *An heroic feat with dead men* (*Disasters* Plate 39)

53 *Rightly or wrongly* (*Disasters* Plate 2)

54 *The worst is to beg* (*Disasters* Plate 55)

55 *Appeals are in vain* (*Disasters* Plate 54)

56 *What is the use of a cup?* (*Disasters* Plate 59)

57 *Nothing. That is what it says* (*Disasters* Plate 69)

58   *That is the worst of it!* (*Disasters* Plate 74)

59   *The carnivorous vulture* (*Disasters* Plate 76)

forebodings of what is to come'. This plate, together with several others added to the war and famine scenes and fifteen plates at the end of the series, including Plates 81 and 82, are all etched on a uniform group of copperplates, and their preparatory drawings are also on one distinctive type of paper. Most of them are savage satires against the Church and the *camarilla* which were responsible for the appalling reaction under Ferdinand, restored as absolute monarch on the throne of Spain in May 1814. These are the *caprichos enfáticos* of the title in the Ceán Bermúdez album, but amongst them is a print which appears to link the disasters of the Napoleonic period to the even more 'fatal consequences' of Ferdinand's return.

57   Plate 69 of the *Disasters of War* has the number engraved in both the top and bottom corners, suggesting that it may have been intended as a postscript to the war and famine scenes. The dark, grainy aquatint makes it difficult to distinguish all the elements of the composition, but an early proof in pure etching shows that the corpse rising from his grave to inscribe the word *Nada*, 'Nothing', on a sheet of paper, is turning his back on the figure of Justice, whose scales are still visible in the final aquatinted state. A horde of flying demons hovers over the corpse, coming between Justice and the dead man who clutches a wicker crown. The demons' leader, whose dress suggests a monk's or cleric's gown, shouts imprecations and points upwards, but into the darkness, away from the almost obliterated rays of light coming from the area where Justice now appears to be supporting a frail figure – Truth, perhaps, or the Constitution (as a recent analysis suggests). The etched inscription *Nada* in the print is echoed in Goya's manuscript title on the proof in the Ceán album: *Nada. Ello lo dice*, 'Nothing. That is what it says'. The mid-nineteenth-century Academicians apparently found this too nihilistic, and when the title was engraved on the plate, Goya's pessimistic affirmation was altered to the more ambiguous *Ello dirá*, 'Time will tell'.

This print has been compared with an engraving by Otto Van Veen in a seventeenth-century emblem book. Goya apparently knew the edition published in Brussels in 1669 and 1672 with a Spanish text, since there are references to Van Veen's imagery in drawings made in Madrid *c*.1820 and Goya incorporated a poem from the book in a late drawing made in Bordeaux. Van Veen's allegorical image of Death appears as the final plate in the *Teatro moral de toda la filosofía* 'for the education of kings and princes'. Goya's corpse-like figure which half-rises from the grave shares with Van Veen's skeleton of a king the attribute of the crown and the scales of Justice, suggesting that Goya intended an allegory on Ferdinand VII's abuse of power and abandonment of justice and the Constitution. By now it was clear to the disillusioned liberals and to the nation that at the end of the long years of war and suffering their king had brought them 'Nothing', although he, too, would find nothing but death and darkness at the end.

In a single year, the king set aside the Constitution and all its reforms, reintroduced the old systems of government, restored the Inquisition, reopened the suppressed monasteries and convents, and finally recalled the Jesuits whom his grandfather, Charles III, had expelled from Spain in 1766. All who were suspected of liberal sympathies were persecuted and freedom of the press was abolished. The measures taken were so extreme that they led to increasing discontent in the country and to abortive plots, mutinies and revolutionary activity. At the beginning of 1820, a rising under Rafael de Riego forced the king to swear loyalty to the Constitution and for three years there was an uneasy but hopeful period of liberal government. Goya must have hoped to be able to publish his set of prints at this time. To the war and famine prints and the dark *Nada* plate he added the *caprichos enfáticos* whose date is uncertain and which were possibly not completed until the Constitution was restored in 1820.

60 *Will she [Truth] rise again?* (*Disasters* Plate 80)

61 *This is the true way* (*Disasters* Plate 82)

It has been suggested that '*caprichos enfáticos*' can be taken, if the adjective 'emphatic' is interpreted in its eighteenth-century rhetorical sense, to mean that these prints 'make a point or give a warning by insinuation rather than by direct statement', that is, are 'allegorical' rather than 'striking' as the term has usually been translated. Allegory and fable have long been recognised as the basis of their imagery and recently a source for a number of the prints has been identified in a satirical verse fable by Giambattista Casti. His poem *Gli animali parlanti*, 'The talking animals', was first published in 1802 (Casti died in 1803 and Goya made a commemorative drawing of him) and it was at least

58 partially translated into Spanish by 1813. In Plate 74, an almost direct quotation of a line of Casti's poem is inscribed by a wolf on a sheet of paper together with Casti's name. Casti's wolf is a cruel and deceitful minister who at this point in the poem is concerned with the crushing of a revolution. The quotation 'Miserable humanity, the fault is thine' lays the blame for their rulers' barbarity on the victims' own acceptance of it. The victim appears on the left with his hands bound, while a monk kneels before the wolf, holding out the inkwell. Plate 77, which shows a white horse fighting a pack of wolves, watched by a group of passive wolf hounds, can also be related to Casti's poem in which the horse is a symbol of constitutional monarchy which fights off the wolves, the king's corrupt and cruel ministers, but without enlisting the help of the dogs who would represent the forces of anti-monarchist revolution.

This print precedes Plates 79 and 80 in which an allegorical figure identified as Truth

60 dies, surrounded by threatening clerical figures, but continues in the following plate to radiate light, despite the blows aimed at her by monks and monsters. It has been suggested that this figure, who is clothed and wears a laurel wreath, is not strictly a personification of Truth, who should appear naked, and has more in common with the figures identified as personifications of the Constitution of Spain in an allegorical painting of *c*.1812–13 (Nationalmuseum, Stockholm) and in the portrait of Ferdinand VII painted for the Municipality of Santander in 1814. If this is so, a new unity is given to the etchings at the end of Goya's series. The horse and the allegorical figures in Plates

61 79, 80 and 82 would all refer to Spanish constitutional monarchy which Goya, like so many liberal patriots, must have wished to uphold.

It is tempting to extend this interpretation to all the 'allegorical *caprichos*'. In Plate 65, the dishevelled, weeping woman in white could symbolise the Constitution rejected by Ferdinand in 1814. The next three plates are satirical allegories on the power of the

57 reactionary, clerical forces behind the king who in Plate 69 is shown rejecting Justice and good government, urged on by the fanatical *camarilla*. The people of Spain wander blindly through a wasteland (Plate 70) and the forces of evil reign supreme and appear to dominate the world (Plate 71). In the following plates Casti's vampires, cats, owls and wolves hold sway, with the support of the clergy who are revealed in Plate 75 as a 'Troupe of charlatans'. But the people are roused from their torpor and the passive resignation deplored by Casti. As they fought the French soldiers with pitchforks and

53, 59 axes in 1808, so a Spanish patriot, cheered on by a crowd, attacks a 'carnivorous vulture', the tattered symbol of misrule, which struggles away, 'excreting' an ecclesiastical figure in a gross visual pun, while 'bourgeois' figures to the right turn and run (Plate 76). In the plate which precedes the final allegories on the fight, death and final triumph of good government, a cardinal or bishop (prudently reduced from the status of Pope given to him in the preparatory drawing) sways on a frayed rope above the heads of the crowd, with the comment 'The cord is going to break' (Plate 77). The final image

61 is one of peace and plenty as a radiant figure indicates to an aged peasant the natural riches of the land, with the caption *Esto es lo verdadero*, 'This is the true way' (Plate 82).

In these extraordinary plates, the visions of the artist, now seventy-five years old, are expressed with masterly freedom and subtlety. The almost rough technique and splendid vigour of the later war and famine scenes develop a breadth of design and handling characteristic of the late work of the greatest masters. The line sums up gesture and expression or flickers round the forms suggesting the sway of contending forces. Fluid acid washes and a brilliant improvisation with accidental tones highlight the apparition of virtue or add veils of darkness to the plates whose images express Goya's deepest emotions in the face of every threat to the freedoms he had always believed in.

5 The Tauromaquia

The set of prints of bullfighting subjects, which Goya advertised for sale in October and December 1816, appears to come as a respite between his etchings of the horrors of war and those of the *caprichos enfáticos* which probably reflect the years of Ferdinand's absolute rule between 1814 and 1820. The Tauromaquia series is, however, far from being as simple as the description on the explanatory sheet suggests: 'Thirty-three prints which represent different *suertes* [manoeuvres] and actions in the art of bullfighting, invented and etched in Madrid by Don Francisco de Goya y Lucientes'. There follows a list of titles for the etchings, titles that were not engraved on the plates themselves. These cover the history of bullfighting from its origins in the hunting of bulls by the ancient Spaniards, through the development of the art of contesting with bulls, initiated by the Moors during their occupation of Spain and perfected by Christian princes and noblemen, until it was finally taken over by the common people in the eighteenth century and became a popular sport whose heroes were applauded and idolised by the crowds for the intelligence and agility, the elegance and daring of their performance.

The titles of the printed explanatory sheet are known in two further versions, which differ from each other. Goya's own manuscript titles, which are in general much briefer, have been identified on a set of the prints in the Boston Public Library. A third set of titles, intermediary between the other two, is found in the album which was given by Goya, as was his usual practice, to Ceán Bermúdez. Two notes by Carderera, who later owned this volume, record Goya's intention that Ceán should 'write out the title and the legends' and the fact that 'the numbers are written on pasted pieces of paper and the explanation is written by the son of Ceán Bermúdez as his father dictated it'. Ceán's leather-bound volume (now part of the Tomás Harris collection in the British Museum)
43 is lettered TOROS DE GOYA on the spine and has a carefully designed manuscript title-
62 page, lettered in ink and similar in style to that of Ceán's album of war prints. The wording of this title page was followed at the head of the explanatory sheet for the first edi-
64 tion. The following sheet has a manuscript list of 'Subjects of the Prints', written out according to the new order which Ceán had given them; Ceán in fact not merely rearranged the plates but scratched out the numbers that Goya had etched on them, sticking large tabs with his new numbers in manuscript to the top centre of every print.
76 The list includes an additional print, number 34, *Modo de volar*, 'A way of flying', which is also described on the manuscript title-page as 'the way in which men can fly with
63 wings'. Pasted on to the middle of the page facing the list of plates, as a frontispiece, is a proof of a small etching representing a blind guitarist tossed by a bull. It has a manuscript title, probably in Goya's hand, *Barbara diversion!*, 'Barbarous entertainment!', and below is an inscription (in pencil, but closely resembling the ink calligraphy of the list of prints) *Esta es la voz del Publico racional, religioso e ilustrado de España*, 'This is the voice of the rational, religious and enlightened People of Spain'.

These titles, alterations and additional prints raise fascinating questions concerning the artist's intentions and the ideas of Ceán and perhaps other friends with whom Goya

Treinta y tres Estampas.
que representan diferentes suertes y actitudes
del arte de lidiar los Toros;
y una el modo de poder volar los hombres con alas.

Inventadas, diseñadas y grabadas al agua fuerte
por el Pintor original
D. Francisco de Goya y Lucientes

En Madrid.

Este exemplar es el que Goya entregó a D. Ag.ᵈ Ceán Bermudez p.ᵃ redactar el titulo y epigrafes. Así, es unico por estar sin los numeros q.ᵉ en los exemplares comunes hay grabados; además hay hechos precisos en su persona, respectos, y tienen diferente colocación los exemplares. Es también antes de las letras q.ᵉ se escribe pegado al reverso no escrita en la edición el epígrafe de mano de Goya

62 Title-page of the Ceán album of the *Tauromaquia*

Barbara diversion

63 *Barbarous entertainment!* Proof mounted in the Ceán *Tauromaquia* album (*opposite*, 64)

65–7 Details of Plates 1, 11 and 30 of the *Tauromaquia*

Asuntos de las Estampas.

1. El modo con que los antiguos españoles cazaban los Toros á caballo en el campo.

2. Otro modo de cazarles á pie.

3. Los Moros establecidos en España, prescindiendo de las supersticiones de su Alcoran, adoptaron esta caza y arte.

4. Comienzan los Moros á capear los Toros en cercado con el albornoz.

5. Otro capeo de Toros, hecho por los Moros en plaza.

6. Los Moros torean con harpones ó banderillas.

7. Un Moro es cogido del Toro, lidiando con banderillas.

8. El saliente moro Gazul lanzeó con galantería y destreza.

9. El Cid campeador, el primer Caballero español que alanceó los Toros con esfuerzo.

10. Otro Caballero español, despues de haber perdido el Caballo, mata el Toro á pie con suma gallardía.

11. Palenque que hacia la Canalla con burros para defenderse de los Toros.

12. Carlos V mata un Toro de una lanzada en la plaza de Valladolid en las fiestas de Toros, que se celebraron allí por el nacimiento de su hijo Felipe II.

13. Un Caballero en plaza quebrando rejoncillos.

14. Desparece de la Canalla con lanzas, medias-lunas banderillas y otras armas.

15. El diestrísimo y famoso Estudiante de Falces, embozado burlando al Toro con sus quiebros.

16. El insigne Martincho poniendo banderillas al quiebro.

17. Temeridad del mismo Martincho en la plaza de Madrid.

18. Otra locura del propio Martincho en la de Zaragoza.

19. El esforzado Mamon cuela un Toro en la de Madrid.

20. Ligereza y atrevimiento de Juanito Apiñani, alias el de Calahorra tambien en la de Madrid.

21. Desgracias acaecidas en el tendido de esta plaza, y muerte del Alcalde de Torrejon.

22. Valor varonil de la celebre Pajuelera en la de Zaragoza.

23. Mariano Ceballos, alias el Indio mata el Toro desde su caballo.

24. El mismo Ceballos quiebra rejones montado sobre otro Toro, en la de Madrid.

25. Caída de un Picador de su caballo debaxo del Toro.

26. El celebre Fernando del Toro barilarguero obligando á la fiera con su garrocha.

27. El esforzado Rendon que murió en esta suerte en la plaza de Madrid.

28. Perros.

29. Banderillas de fuego.

30. Dos grupos de Picadores arrollados en el suelo de seguida por un solo Toro.

31. Pedro Romero matando el Toro parado.

32. Pepe-Illo, haciendo al Toro el recorte.

33. Su desgraciada muerte en la plaza de Madrid.

34. Modo de volar.

64 List of 'Subjects of the Prints' (with different numbering) in the Ceán *Tauromaquia* album

discussed his project. Goya's original title for the series was simply *Fiestas de Toros*, 'Bullfights', which appeared as part of his manuscript title on the first plate on the Boston proofs: *Origen de las fiestas de Toros. Grabadas a la agua fuerte p^r. Dⁿ. Fran^{co} Goya, Pintor de Cam^a del Rey*, 'The origin of Bullfights. Etched by Don Francisco Goya, Court Painter to the King'. His titles to the plates are equally short and pithy, similar in this respect to those of the *Caprichos* and of the war and famine prints. They even include a typical dramatisation of a particularly violent and tragic scene, with the comment 'I saw it' (Plate 21). But did Goya originally set out to make a didactic, historical account of the art of bullfighting, with possibly satirical and allegorical intentions, as the additional prints and their titles in Ceán's album suggest?

The advertisements published in the *Diario* and the *Gazeta de Madrid* describe these prints as illustrations of 'various *suertes* with bulls, and events which have occurred in connection with these performances in our bullrings; the set of prints gives an idea of the origins, development and present state of these bullfights in Spain, which is apparent even without an explanation, simply from looking at the prints'. If the whole series was considered easy to understand 'even without an explanation', Goya must have intended it for *aficionados* who, like himself, would have had no difficulty in identifying the memorable or legendary events portrayed. Occasionally in his titles, Goya indicated the names, usually nicknames, of the bullfighters: 'Martincho', 'Mamón', 'La Pajuelera', Pedro Romero and 'Pepe Hillo', but more often he simply described the pass or *suerte* and apparently expected the viewer to identify the torero or the particular occasion.

Goya began the series with the etchings of contemporary scenes in the bullring. Three prints are signed and dated 1815 and these, as well as the many rejected or accidentally damaged plates (excluded from the first published edition) show the kind of spectacular and dramatic incidents which Goya had enjoyed with the crowds in the bullrings at Madrid and Saragossa. The unity of this first group of prints is underlined by the fact that all the preparatory drawings are on the same, distinctive type of paper. The historical prints followed later; many were etched on the back of discarded or damaged plates of the modern bullring scenes, and in them Goya's style went through its characteristic development from compositions full of figures in realistic settings to powerfully condensed and abstracted images, where a man and a bull often appear alone, with no more than a hint of a barrier or the patterns of light and shade on the empty floor of the arena. This is clearly seen in the cases where Goya repeated the design of an abandoned plate, always simplifying and strengthening the effect of the composition. He gave the historical plates the briefest of titles which evoke the origin of a particular *suerte* or the name of a legendary figure, such as the moor Gazul, El Cid, and the Emperor Charles v. However, when Goya put his plates into order and etched the numbers, their sequence was far from logical or historically correct, the most glaring error being the placing of the sixteenth-century Charles v before the eleventh-century El Cid.

Ceán Bermúdez's aim in changing the order of the plates and their numbers and dictating lengthy explanatory titles was evidently to produce a more logical and instructive publication for a public which knew less about the technicalities of bull-fighting than the seventy-year-old Goya and his fellow *aficionados*, but which could be expected to appreciate a well-informed and properly documented historical account of Spain's national sport. But Ceán, presumably with Goya's consent, went further and apparently decided that the series should not only provide information about the history and modern practice of bullfighting but should also express a moral judgement (in the additional frontispiece plate) and give an allegorical interpretation of the whole series (in the tail-piece of the 'Flying men'). That this was probably Ceán's initiative is suggested

68 *The Moors make a different play in the ring calling the bull with their burnous* (*Tauromaquia* Plate 6)

69 As 68, but with addition of aquatint

70 *Another way of hunting on foot* (*Tauromaquia* Plate 2)

71 *Charles V spearing a bull in the ring at Valladolid* (*Tauromaquia* Plate 10)

by the fact that the album was put together and bound after he had altered the numbers of the prints and had drafted the legends which were so different from Goya's own. In the event, Goya did not accept the idea of renumbering the plates, the titles as published were somewhat simplified, and the provocative frontispiece and the tail-piece with its allegorical implications were dropped from the sequence.

What were the precedents for such a series of prints? Why did Goya undertake such a project at this stage in his career? And how far did he go along with his scholarly friend's enthusiasm for an historical and moralising account of this spectacular subject? By the 1790s, bullfighting was a highly popular and fashionable entertainment. The Duchesses of Alba and Osuna supported rival matadors and everyone flocked to the Monday bull-fights which were so frequently mentioned in Goya's letters to Zapater. In 1805 the sport had been banned by Charles IV but the ban was relaxed in 1810 by Joseph Bonaparte, probably in the hope of winning some popular support. By 1815 bullfighting had become the symbol of a nationalistic, patriotic attitude, and was celebrated in numerous prints and literary publications. But more enlightened circles, in which Goya came to have many friends and acquaintances, were generally repelled by what they regarded as a barbarous and unedifying spectacle. In the famous pamphlet *Pan y Toros*, 'Bread and Bulls', which appeared in 1796, the bullfight and its audience were seen as a symbol of all that was most vicious and degrading in Spanish society, from the highest to the lowest classes, and this view was no doubt shared by Ceán and the younger Moratín.

In 1790 Antonio Carnicero published a set of twelve prints illustrating the different phases of a bullfight. The clear, somewhat naïve designs proved a great success with the public and were frequently imitated. In 1796 the name of one of the most famous matadors, Pepe Hillo, was given as the author of a handbook on bullfighting published in Cadiz. A later, expanded edition included thirty rather crude illustrations whose chief interest lies in the fact that, unlike Carnicero's series, they also gave a historical view of bullfighting on which Goya seems to have based some of his prints. When Goya planned or was encouraged by Ceán to add a comprehensive historical section to his bullfight prints, he also made use of another work, the short history of bullfighting written by the father of his friend Moratín and published in 1777. The idea of adding illustrations of 'the origin and development' of bullfighting provided Goya with an opportunity to make an

70 extraordinarily rich use of his fantasy and imagination as he recreated scenes of ancient
65, 68 Spaniards in the open country, of elegant and fearless 'Moors' (directly derived from the Egyptian Mamelukes who formed one of the most ferocious elements in Napoleon's
66, 71 army in Spain), as well as of knights of old in costumes whose incongruity has often been noted.

The series as finally published was put on sale in a print shop in the Calle Mayor at 10 reales for individual plates or 300 reales for the set of thirty-three. It seems to have met with little success and the reasons are not difficult to understand. Compared with the normal stock of print dealers and bookshops – decorative illustrations of 'cries' and customs, costume prints or bullfight scenes like those by Carnicero and his imitators, sold plain or gaily hand-coloured – Goya's etched and aquatinted plates must have appeared unpolished and incomprehensible. Goya's prints have neither the naïve simplicity of Carnicero's rather wooden scenes, nor the circumstantial detail and high finish expected of realistic, illustrative works. Each plate presents a dramatic moment in a particular encounter between a wild and dangerous bull and men whose emotions, or their proud control of them, are written on their faces or expressed in the turn and thrust of their bodies. The primitive intelligence of the 'ancient Spaniards', the superior cunning and supple grace of the Moors, the majestic appearance and courage of the plumed and armoured Christian princes and noblemen, and finally the down-to-earth bravery and skill of the professional toreros of Goya's time, all these are shown in a way 65–7 which emphasises the tension and drama of each contest. Details from three prints, of an 'ancient Spaniard', the medieval knight El Cid and Goya's great contemporary, the matador Pedro Romero, show not only the highly individualised character of the figures but also the masterly freedom and expressive qualities of the artist's etching line. The infinitely varied character of the etched line and the subtle or dramatic use of aquatint tones convey the images in an impressionistic, even expressionist, form which must have been beyond the comprehension of the ordinary public and even of the more enlightened collectors whom Goya and Ceán no doubt wished to interest.

70 A subtly balanced, asymmetrical composition shows ancient Spaniards spearing a bull (Plate 2). The figures are set in a shadowy landscape, suggested by delicately modulated aquatint tones which cover lightly etched trees and bushes in the distance. The desperate concentration and firm stance of the hunters with their still dangerous prey recall the intensity of the struggles between Spanish patriots and French soldiers in some of the war prints and the *caprichos enfáticos* on which Goya was probably already working 53, 59 at this time (*Desastres* Plates 2 and 76). This etching was made on the back of one of the seven rejected designs which were later included in the third and subsequent editions of this series.

All the prints were made from preparatory drawings in red chalk, which were transferred to the copperplate in Goya's normal way and then freely interpreted with 68 the etching needle. A proof in pure etching of one of the prints, showing Moors playing the bull with a burnous (Plate 6), differs markedly from the drawing. Where the nearest Moor was originally dressed in a long, dark robe and the burnous, held behind him, was visible above as well as below the sleeves of his caftan, in the proof, Goya's change of design is visible in the tentative outline of the skirt between the Moor's legs and in the strong burnishing marks which remain where the burnous was removed over his left arm. In this proof, the stone wall and stockade with watching figures and the shadows on 69 the ground form arbitrary, abstract patterns, balancing the two men and the bull in the foreground. The veil of aquatint then applied to the plate and lightly burnished around the main protagonists throws them into relief and obscures the fascinating but distracting background elements. In the printing of the edition, the touches of drypoint on the nearer figure's dress lost their rich burr and print thinly, showing up a gap in the etched lines of the fringe. This plate, too, was etched on the verso of an earlier, abandoned design.

71 The representation of the Emperor Charles V spearing a bull during the fiestas held at Valladolid to celebrate the birth of his son in 1527 was referred to in the text of Nicolás Fernández de Moratín in terms which Ceán repeated almost word for word in his manuscript title, elaborating on Goya's lapidary 'Charles the fifth, in the ring at Valladolid' (Plate 10). There is, in fact, a total absence of setting in this print, one of the boldest and most unconventional in the series. The composition created by the re-lationship of the mounted king, the bull and the direction of the lance was worked out in no fewer than three drawings. In the final image, powerful thrusting and turning movements are contained within the compact, monumental group which is balanced against the abstract gradation of the aquatint tones to the right.

72 One of the early prints, signed and dated 1815, shows the matador known as Martincho preparing to leap from a table over the bull's back, with his legs in irons (Plate 19). It is a good example of the earlier type of composition in which groups of

72 *Another madness of his [Martincho] in the same ring [at Saragossa]* (*Tauromaquia* Plate 19)

73 *Mariano Ceballos, called the Indian, kills the bull from his horse* (*Tauromaquia* Plate 23)

74 *The agility and audacity of Juanito Apiñani in the ring at Madrid* (*Tauromaquia* Plate 20)

75 *Dreadful events in the front rows of the ring at Madrid and death of the mayor of Torrejón* (*Tauromaquia* Plate 21)

figures, here already simplified in comparison with the preparatory drawing, are placed in front of the barrier above which a densely-packed crowd is indicated, shaded with heavy, horizontal hatching. As in all the early plates, there is only a single, etched borderline. In this print Goya named only the exploit, not the torero, but he is identified in Ceán's legend and on the printed title page. On another print, Goya's manuscript title refers to his fellow countryman with pride as *El famoso Aragones Martincho*.

74   In the following print (Plate 20) the perfectly balanced figure of Juanito Apiñani vaults effortlessly over the horns of the bull which gallops at full stretch across the arena. In this somewhat later plate, framed by a broad etched border, the setting is simplified and the isolated bull and torero are balanced by the lively shapes, some lit and some in shade, of the sketchy but clearly individualised onlookers under their parasols.

     Goya, whose visual memory was phenomenal and who knew as well as anyone what a bullring looked like, was totally uninterested in the depiction of inessential elements. The relative positions of a man and a bull were 'correct' to the extent that they expressed the physical and psychological trial of strength between them. But the incidental activities, the costumes and the depiction of the bullring itself, were never of any particular concern to Goya. A print by Carnicero showing the Madrid bullring in 1791 clearly distinguishes the different elements which should make up the background of Goya's prints: the wooden barrier with its low ledge which the toreros used for jumping into and out of the ring, then the corridor round which they could run, bounded by another, higher barrier with posts and cords to protect the common people seated in the front rows of the wooden stands which rise steeply towards the covered balconies occupied by the gentry.

     Goya's onlookers – whom he shows only in the *tendido*, the front rows – often appear to lean directly over the bullring barrier, leaving no space for the *callejón*, or corridor, and there is never any indication of the ropes which had been added to the ring in Madrid in

75 1784. Plate 21, one of the most dramatic and moving in the whole series, shows an incident said to have occurred in the ring at Madrid in 1801 and which the ropes were intended to prevent. The scene recalls the horrors of the war and Goya's manuscript title is as abrupt and dramatic as any on those prints: *Salto el toro al tendido, y mato a dos. Yo lo vi*, 'The bull jumped into the front rows and killed two people. I saw it'. Ceán's more circumstantial title, copied in the printed title page, identifies the dead man impaled on the bull's horns as the mayor of Torrejón. The composition, chaotic and overcrowded in the preparatory drawing, is here reduced to a tautly expressive, daringly off-centre contrast between the empty seats on the left and the violent movement of the figures fleeing from the motionless bull which stands silhouetted with his tragic human burden against the empty arena. A curious lavis border was added round the composition which is the only one showing a view from the stands down into the ring.

     Goya's decision to make an ambitious set of prints on this theme has to be seen in relation to his personal and professional situation. Early in 1814, he had petitioned the Regency Council for support for a project to make paintings depicting 'our glorious insurrection against the tyrant of Europe', hastening to add that he was in a 'state of absolute penury' and would require financial assistance. His request was granted and he was allowed a monthly pension as well as any expenses incurred during his depiction of the *Dos de mayo* and *Tres de mayo 1808*. Goya must have hoped to publish his prints of the 'fatal consequences' of Spain's war against the 'tyrant' Bonaparte at this time. However, with the return of Ferdinand and the resulting repression, this project could not be realised. Although a number of town councils and other corporate bodies commissioned portraits of the restored monarch and some of his ministers from Goya, the First Court

76 *A way of flying* (*Proverbios* Plate 13). Proof bound in the Ceán *Tauromaquia* album (as Plate 34)

77 As 76, but with addition of aquatint

78 Untitled folly (*Proverbios* Plate 10)

79 As 78, but with addition of aquatint

Painter never received a commission from the king himself. Moreover, as a member of the royal household, Goya was subject to a rigorous vetting before payment of his salary could be resumed. His case, supported by the testimony of witnesses, was examined in November and December 1814 and Goya was able to prove that he had not collaborated with the enemy, that he had not touched his salary under the intruder government and had never worn the decoration awarded to him by Joseph Bonaparte. One of the witnesses in his 'purification' process testified that from the beginning of the French occupation of Madrid, Goya had lived 'withdrawn in his house and studio, devoting himself to painting and engraving', and Goya himself maintained that he had sold his jewels cheaply rather than accept anything from the intruders.

An entry in the diary of the Swedish envoy to Madrid, who visited Goya's house in the Calle de Valverde in July 1815, throws a fascinating light on his situation at this period. Referring to the almost deaf artist, now threatened by blindness 'which does not, however affect his satirical vein', he added that Goya was 'living in straightened circumstances . . . attributable to his curious state of mind and caprices', having one day given away 'his whole fortune, which was considerable, to his son and daughter-in-law'. This helps to explain Goya's reference to his 'state of absolute penury' in 1814, despite the fact that, after his wife's death in 1812, he retained a half share of their very substantial common property (all recorded in an inventory before its division with his son). It is also worth recalling that Goya was in trouble with the Inquisition in 1815 on account of two 'immoral and abominable' paintings – the naked and clothed *Majas* – which were among the pictures in the confiscated collections of Ferdinand's most hated enemy, Godoy.

In these circumstances, Goya's project to etch and publish a set of bullfight prints may be compared with his activity after his illness in 1792, when, as he explained to Iriarte, he made his set of little cabinet pictures (including several bullfighting scenes), 'in order to occupy my imagination mortified by the contemplation of my sufferings and to compensate in part for the considerable expense which they have caused me'. The pension and expenses granted by the Regency Council and the various official commissions he received apparently enabled Goya to purchase a very large quantity of the best quality copperplates, imported from London, which he used for the etchings of the *Tauromaquia* and the later *Disparates* series. In 1815 Goya painted a superb portrait of Rafael Esteve, a Valencian friend who was an expert engraver and printer. Esteve had just returned to Madrid after ten years of travel in Europe and it is very possible that he helped Goya with the printing and the aquatinting of the *Tauromaquia* plates. The beautiful aquatint effects of the later plates and the quality of the printed edition as a whole are very close to the *Caprichos* with which Esteve may also have been involved. With Esteve's technical assistance and expertise and with the encouragement and enthusiasm of the faithful Ceán, Goya probably worked with a variety of aims on his newest print project.

In terms of their style and content, the *Tauromaquia* prints are very close to the paintings of the *Dos* and *Tres de mayo 1808*: the bulls are lacking, but the horses, the 'Moors', the brave fighters on foot and the dead and wounded are all present in the first painting, while the firmer, more dramatic groupings of the second provide a formal counterpart to the mature balance and sure handling of the later bullfight scenes. What of any possible hidden connotations, satirical or allegorical, in Goya's *Tauromaquia* prints? Can the bull be seen as a symbol of the blind forces of ignorance and brutality which brave and ardent fighters, from the dawn of Spain's history to the present time, have
63 combated with exemplary valour? Is the 'Barbarous entertainment!' of the frontispiece in

Ceán's album intended as a criticism of the people who enjoy the brutal spectacle or of the bull which tosses a personification of poor, blind Spain on his horns? Goya's ironic title on the preparatory drawing for this print, *Dios se lo pague a usted*, 'May God reward you', shows the blind beggar unaware of his danger as he politely thanks the bull, mistaking him for someone who wishes to help him. The longer title below the print in Ceán's album is as ambiguous as Goya's title on the print itself. The same can be said of
76 the additional print at the end of the volume, showing 'the way in which men can fly with wings'. Some have interpreted this as a pessimistic fantasy on the futility of man's efforts, others see it as a natural extension of the power of rational, intelligent man to solve all problems and overcome all obstacles. But whatever the ideas and intentions of Goya and Ceán, it would have been too dangerous to suggest a hidden meaning in the prints and they were published as a purely historical and documentary series. Goya's private views were expressed in the drawings which he continued to add to his 'journal albums', in the *caprichos enfáticos* with which he completed his etchings of the war, and in the visions and fantasies of the *Disparates* prints.

80 *Fools' folly* (additional plate for *Proverbios*)

81 *Brute folly* (additional plate for *Proverbios*)

6 The Proverbios or Disparates

After the publication of his bullfighting prints in October 1816, Goya continued to make etchings on the large English copperplates which he had acquired. One of the earliest, if 76 not the first, of the new prints was the 'Way of flying' which Ceán Bermúdez had included at the end of his album of the bullfighting subjects. It belongs to a group of twenty-two prints which Goya probably executed between 1816 and 1823 and which are the most powerful, original and enigmatic of his works in etching and aquatint. The years of their creation would cover the period during which Ferdinand's repressive, absolute rule continued, until an uprising in 1820 forced him to accept the Constitution of Cadiz and introduced three years of shaky, constitutional government. This period of renewed liberal hopes ended abruptly when the Duc d'Angoulême led a French expedition into Spain and restored Ferdinand to power. At the beginning of 1819, Goya bought a house, known as the Quinta del Sordo, on the outskirts of Madrid. He left the house in the Calle de Valverde, which already belonged, with many of his paintings, to his son, and went to live in his new home with the young woman who had probably been his companion since his wife's death in 1812 and who remained with him until his own death in Bordeaux in 1828.

Goya decorated the main rooms in the Quinta with strange murals, the celebrated 'black paintings', and he continued to work on his drawings and prints until the French invasion. When the success of the French army appeared inevitable, after the destruction at Trocadero of the defences of Cadiz, Goya made the Quinta over as a gift to his grandson in September 1823. After the execution of Riego and the triumph of Ferdinand, the repression which followed was so harsh that from January to April 1824 Goya went into hiding with a friend who held official government posts but helped and protected the endangered liberals. On 1 May an amnesty for the liberals was declared and on the following day Goya presented a petition to the king, requesting six months' leave, with full pay, to take the waters at Plombières in France. He left Spain on 24 June.

After Goya's death, an inventory listed the works owned by his son. It included 'Two cases of engravings and drawings, aquatints, *caprichos*, etc. Three books of original, unpublished drawings. Four cartons of engravings, *caprichos*. Seven cases of objects and copperplates'. All this material had been stored away before Goya left for France and the copperplates included eighty-two unpublished war and allegorical etchings and twenty-two large, unpublished plates of a series of which nothing is certain except that one plate was already etched, if not aquatinted, in 1816 and the series was left incomplete when the plates were packed into cases, probably in the spring or summer of 1823.

Because of the uncertainties surrounding almost every aspect of these prints – their meaning and sequence, the exact dates of their execution and their relationship with the other major works of this period – it may prove helpful to consider the known facts before turning to interpretation and conjecture. There are twenty-two prints as well as at least five additional drawings from which no etchings are known to have been made. Goya used a brush and sanguine wash (over the lightest of indications in red chalk) for all the preparatory drawings which are breathtaking in their freedom and vitality. Many of them are so broadly handled that the elements of their composition are barely recognisable, and in most cases Goya extensively altered his original idea when he drew with his etching needle over the faint traces of the transferred drawing on the copperplate. Sometimes the alterations were so drastic that several drawings were not or may still not have been recognised as the preparatory studies for a particular print.

For at least seven of the prints, no preparatory drawings are known. Because the series was incomplete when Goya left Spain, the only contemporary impressions from the plates are the few working proofs which have survived (generally only one or two from each plate and in four cases none at all). Of four prints, proofs are known only before the addition of aquatint. Of the more numerous proofs with aquatint, thirteen have a title in ink and usually a number. There has been much discussion as to whether the titles are Goya's and were inscribed by him on the proofs, but it is now generally accepted that this is the case. The titles all begin with the word *Disparate*, meaning 'Folly', characterised by an adjective or a phrase which is often evocative but certainly not enlightening: 'Cruel folly', 'Merry folly', 'Clear folly', 'Carnival folly', for example.

This latter title, however, suggests a clue to the series as a whole. Many of the prints have been shown to represent carnival themes and it is quite possible that Goya used Carnival as an allegory through which to express complex ideas which may include particular as well as general allusions to the state of Spain and to his personal and private world which, since the time of the *Caprichos*, had always been intermingled in his works of '*capricho* and invention'.

76   The print of the 'Flying men' was included in a state before the addition of aquatint in Ceán Bermúdez's album of the *Tauromaquia*. Despite its symbolic overtones, it was probably based on an actual attempted flight and has been compared with a print illustrating the machine which Jacob Degen 'flew', with the aid of a balloon, in Vienna in 1808. This type of exploit, 'flying' and the ascent of balloons, was associated with fairs and carnivals, and a fantastic, Spanish variation was recorded in 1784 by Isidro Carnicero in a print showing a bull and mounted bullfighter suspended from balloons. One of Goya's late drawings, made in Bordeaux, shows a flying bull accompanied by a balloon-like cluster of butterfly-winged heads. Its title, 'They fly, they fly. Fiesta in the air',

80 could be applied to another print from the *Disparates* series, showing a group of topsy-turvy bulls suspended in space. The unique contemporary proof is inscribed *Disparate de tontos*, 'Fools' folly'. This is one of four plates that became separated from the eighteen published by the Academy of San Fernando in 1864, and which were first published in France in 1877.

If these two prints, with their more realistic style, are obviously closely related to Goya's *Fiestas de Toros* and extend the idea of the fiesta into flights of fantasy, many of the other *Disparate* prints and drawings are explicitly or implicitly related to the festive celebrations of the pre- or mid-Lent Carnival. They show the tossing of a man, a donkey and *pelele* figures in a blanket, huge figures on stilts and a dancing giant, human and animal masks, burlesque religious ceremonies and processions, frenzied dancing, dramatic presentations and charades, and many other acts of revelry and resulting scenes of

82 drunkenness and immorality. One of the prints bears the title *Disparate de Carnabal*, 'Carnival folly' (*Proverbios* Plate 14), while another has been shown to be based on an emblematic aspect of Carnival, illustrated in Ripa's *Iconologia* and in a French emblem book where the illustration and accompanying verse are very close to Goya's composition, particularly in the preparatory drawing. In the drawing, an enraptured young woman is plucked up and carried off on the back of a prancing, unbridled horse while the

82 *Carnival folly* (*Proverbios* Plate 14)

83 *Poor folly* (*Proverbios* Plate 11)

84 Untitled folly (*Proverbios* Plate 12)

85 Untitled folly (*Proverbios* Plate 17)

body of a man, who appears to have fallen from the horse, lies to the side. The verse names the horse as *fol vouloir*, 'mad desire', and the girl as 'youth', and alludes to the early destruction of many a young man if the horse has his way. In the print (*Proverbios* Plate 10), the man is omitted but a woman climbs into the mouth of a curious monster who may represent Lasciviousness. The British Museum's proof of the state in pure etching (which once belonged to the great French critic and collector, Philippe Burty) is clear and brilliant, while the aquatint background, although too heavily printed in the posthumous impressions, creates a dramatic atmosphere and highlights the girl's expression and the whiteness of her flesh where the horse has ripped her dress at the shoulder.

81   Carnival is evoked in another allegory which Goya titled *Disparate de Bestia*, 'Brute folly'. No sanguine wash drawing is known and Goya may not even have made one since the elephant was copied from a curious line drawing in pen and sepia ink. This shows two elephants with their keeper, and in the rocky wall to the left of the print, above the white space of the arena, traces of the second elephant are visible. Goya must have decided to eliminate him in the course of work, leaving one of the four Turks or Moors in the foreground still gazing up at the non-existent creature. Warily and with evident alarm, the figures hold up a large book for the elephant to see and proffer a harness with bells.

When these prints were published by the Academy in 1864, they were given the title *Los Proverbios*, possibly because many of the scenes could be identified with proverbs or possibly because the word was also used at that period to refer to an allegory or parable requiring interpretation. Tomás Harris found, in the extraordinarily rich Spanish sources for such material, many proverbs which can be applied to these prints. The huge elephant, the fearful little group of 'wise men' and the cajoling offer of the bell harness suggest a version of the table of the mice who planned to make the cat harmless but then had to decide 'Who will bell the cat?'

How far Goya's allegory has political, religious or social connotations is almost impossible to judge. Among the Carnival themes in the prints the laughing giant of 86 *Proverbios* Plate 4 clicks his castanets and mocks at a man (dressed as a priest in the preparatory drawing) cowering behind an image of a saint or holy virgin. The anticlerical satire and erotic ambiguity are obscured in the final version of this print, in which the grinning giant is the lord of Misrule who upsets the established order and provokes every man to reveal his true nature. Many of the prints, and more clearly still the preparatory drawings, appear to be concerned with the licentious behaviour and 85 immorality of monks and friars. In an untitled *Disparate* print (*Proverbios* Plate 17), friars appear half-undressed in the drawing but the print prudently covers their naked limbs and substitutes a syringe and a strange old man in place of the tall, young victim of the original provocative aggressiveness of their gestures. The changes are so striking between drawing and print that Goya's intentions must have been very precise, even if 83 they remain totally obscure. In *Disparate Pobre*, 'Poor folly' (*Proverbios* Plate 11), a two-headed girl whose voluptuous forms are elegantly clothed in black, looks back towards a cowled figure and at the same time advances with eyes closed towards a group of women, all but one of them old crones, apparently gathered on the steps of a church or convent. A wild figure with hair flying appears in the background and the young woman on the steps gasps in fear. The drawing, however, shows an apparently normal woman pursued by an unidentifiable aggressor and rushing for protection towards a man who could be a soldier wearing a greatcoat. Such alterations make it impossible to take the final state of each print at its face value and any symbolic interpretation has to take all these variations in subject matter into account.

86 Untitled folly (*Proverbios* Plate 4)

87 *Disorderly folly* (*Proverbios* Plate 7)

If more drawings and proofs are discovered (and a number have turned up in recent years), the plan or idea behind the *Disparates* may prove easier to understand. The manuscript numbers on the proofs with *Disparate* titles suggest that Goya was arranging the prints in a sequence where the more obviously allegorical subjects – some of them related to themes which occur in Goya's war scenes and their continuation in the *caprichos enfáticos* – came first. The prints with manuscript numbers 3 to 8 include some of the more violent scenes with anti-clerical or anti-military connotations and the first three of these have the titles 'Cruel', 'Disorderly' and 'Poor folly', in keeping with their themes. Then, after a gap which must be filled by prints without known numbers, prints 16 to 22 include most of the more straightforward representations of Carnival, with titles such as 'Ridiculous', 'Merry', 'Well-known' and 'Carnival folly'.

As the elements in these extraordinary prints are analysed, their kinship with many sources in Goya's own art and with folk customs, emblematic allegory, literary sources and proverbial sayings will be more fully recognised. The closest artistic parallels seem to be on the one hand with Bosch and on the other with Rembrandt. Spanish historians, echoed by Ceán Bermúdez, applied the word *disparate* to Hieronymous Bosch's strange, visionary paintings which were one of the outstanding features of the royal collections in Spain. The emotional intensity in Rembrandt's prints and the structure of his compositions in terms of the gestures and expressions which link the figures, also find an 83 echo in Goya's designs. The *Disparate Pobre*, especially in its preparatory drawing, is remarkably close in feeling as well as in its general composition and individual details to a reversed image of Rembrandt's large *Raising of Lazarus* which Goya may have known or owned. Although the *Disparates*, like the 'black paintings', will probably always remain obscure, their powerful and mysterious images can no longer be regarded as irrational visions, and their significance is beginning to be understood through the unravelling of the artist's creative process.

88 *Don Quixote*, drawing from Album F

7 The Lithographs and Late Etchings

In his study of Goya's drawings published in the *Gazette des Beaux-Arts* in 1860, Valentín Carderera referred to the many drawings unconnected with the series of prints and
88 described a 'Vision of Don Quixote', drawn in brush and ink, which was reproduced in etching by Bracquemond to illustrate his article. This drawing, acquired by the British Museum in 1862, belongs to one of Goya's eight books of drawings, sometimes called 'journal-albums' and now identified by the letters A to H. The albums were broken up, probably by Goya's son, and their pages are now widely scattered in public and private collections throughout the world. The first two albums (A and B, also called the Sanlúcar and Madrid Albums) preceded the *Sueños* drawings and the *Caprichos* prints in the later 1790s, while the last two albums are known to have been made in Bordeaux between 1824 and Goya's death there in 1828. The four intervening albums are more difficult to date, although much of Album C has been shown to be closely related to events in Spain and Goya's preoccupations during the years between 1810 and 1812 when the Constitution of Cadiz was proclaimed. Carderera's article suggests that drawings now mainly identified as belonging to Album F were made in Madrid in about 1819. In 1830, Bartolomé José Gallardo, an old friend of Goya, recalled how the artist had sent word to him when he was in London about an idea he had of making 'some original Caprichos with the title Don Quixote's Visions, in which he portrayed the fantasies of the mad knight of La Mancha in a new style'. The Quixote drawing in the British Museum is page 54 from Album F. It has the appearance of a design for a title-page and
31 recalls Goya's original frontispiece for his *Sueños*, etched as Plate 43 of the *Caprichos*. In the years around 1819, Goya was etching the *Disparates* and there are no other known works on the Quixote theme. Another drawing from the same album was, however, used as the basis for a print in 1819. Pages 10 to 15 of Album F depict men in period costume
90 duelling with swords, and the composition on page 12 was adapted by Goya for one of his earliest lithographs, made in Madrid in February 1819.

Lithography was first introduced into Spain towards the end of 1818 when José María Cardano returned from a year's study of the new technique in Paris and a few months with Senefelder in Munich. He had been sent there on the advice of the director of the Hydrographic Office to which he was attached as a cartographer, and in March 1819 a Royal Order announced the king's decision that the workshop set up in the Institute should function as a public lithographic establishment under the direction of Cardano who had 'just arrived from foreign countries with all the expertise and secrets he had acquired there'. Cardano may have been a good map-maker but he was a poor lithographer. The expensive installation did not prove viable and six years later it was closed down and replaced by a Royal Lithographic Establishment under José de Madrazo. Cardano had meanwhile left Spain and Goya met him again in Paris, shortly before he settled in Bordeaux and produced his celebrated *Bulls of Bordeaux*. The comparison of these masterpieces with Goya's first attempts at lithography in Madrid six years earlier demonstrates his impressive ability, once he was given expert guidance, to adapt a new and barely established technique to his own very personal style and exploit it to produce works which in their assurance and impetuosity have never been surpassed.

Goya's interest in exploiting every technical means at his command is well known. His son Xavier, friends such as Ceán and visitors to his studio reported on his use of the spatula, of split canes which he himself had invented and even of his fingers in the execution of his oil paintings; his drawings are executed in a very wide range of media; and he developed an astonishing range of effects in his use of etching and aquatint. It therefore comes as no surprise that he should have made his way to Cardano's lithographic workshop as soon as it was opened, to investigate the new technique which promised to revolutionise the field of printmaking. In lithography, a drawing is made on stone in a greasy medium, either by pen, wash or crayon. It can be made either directly on the stone or on special transfer paper from which the drawing can be transferred to the stone. So far as the artist is concerned the process is very simple; he simply has to draw, and has none of the worries about grounds and acids that affect etching and aquatint. The complexities of making prints from the drawn stone can be left to the printer. He has to fix the image on the stone and clean it before printing from it by successively wetting and inking it. The grease in the ink of the drawing medium repels the water, which in its turn repels the greasy printing ink; the result is that the ink only settles on the drawing, and can be printed on to a sheet of paper to give a remarkably accurate facsimile of the original.

Goya's first attempt in the new medium, a rather crude pen and ink transfer lithograph, is a study of an old woman spinning, inscribed in the stone *Madrid Febrero 1819*. There is no known contemporary source for the figure which recalls the old spinner in Plate 44 of the *Caprichos*, and the drawing made for transfer has not survived. Goya's early lithographs were all made by the transfer process which Cardano must have demonstrated to him. The results were not very good and few impressions are known. Two of the preparatory drawings have survived and a comparison with the proofs shows that they did not transfer satisfactorily to the stone and that areas of the design failed to

89 print in the lithographs. This is particularly striking in the case of the *Inferno*. The drawing, which belonged to Philippe Burty and was acquired by the British Museum in 1876, is executed in delicate grey ink washes and is very close in style and handling to

88 the *Don Quixote* drawing from Album F; in the unique proof of the lithograph (in the Biblioteca Nacional, Madrid), the lower part of the design failed to print and other areas print weakly or unevenly. This seems to have been partly the fault of Goya who made his drawings on ordinary paper which absorbed much of the ink that should have transferred to the stone, but Cardano's lack of flair must also have contributed to the disappointing results.

Goya's early lithographs are therefore very rare and two are known only from unique impressions. Five impressions, the largest number from any of these stones, are

90 recorded for the *Old style duel* which, according to a lost proof known from a facsimile, was inscribed *Madrid Marzo 1819* and was therefore made in the month following the *Old woman spinning*. Based on the drawing on page 12 from Album F, and redrawn in pen and ink for transfer (the drawing has not survived), this rather bolder design was more successfully printed but all the impressions were retouched by Goya to fill in gaps and strengthen the lithographic image. The British Museum impression (from the Emile Galichon sale in 1875) is retouched in pen and ink in the areas of continuous wash which had printed unevenly. Two other early lithographs (which reflect pairs of fighting figures in Album F) show a young woman in a white dress struggling with a rough-

89 *Inferno*, drawing for a lithograph

90 *Old style duel*

91 *Woman reading*

92 *The Andalusian dance*

looking man. Goya's inscription on one of the proofs, *Espresivo doble fuerza*, 'Expressive of double strength', is obscure but the prints could refer to the common people's blind support of Ferdinand in his overthrow of the Constitution after 1814. Goya made no attempt to publish a series of lithographs and these early prints represent isolated, rather unsatisfactory experiments with a medium that he was later to dominate completely.

In the autumn of 1823, Ferdinand VII again overthrew the liberal, constitutional government of Spain, this time with the help of the French, and the repression which followed apparently forced Goya into hiding at the beginning of the following year. As soon as an amnesty was declared in May, Goya, who was then seventy-eight years old, applied for leave of absence 'to take the curative waters at Plombières' in France. His request was granted and he set out alone, reaching Bayonne on 24 June, where he was given a temporary pass to go to Paris. Three days later he arrived in Bordeaux and was welcomed by his old friend Moratín whose letters to a common friend in Madrid give vivid glimpses of the artist during his last years in France. Moratín's affectionate comments refer to Goya's astonishing vitality and to his impatient and impulsive nature. After only three days' rest in Bordeaux, Goya travelled on to Paris where he stayed for two months.

Ostensibly, Goya went to Paris 'to consult specialists and take the waters that are prescribed for him'. According to a police report, he led a quiet, rather isolated life there, due to his deafness and his difficulty in speaking or understanding French, which prevented his going out except 'to visit monuments and go for walks in public places'. From his own and his friends' letters, however, it is clear that Goya met members of the Spanish emigré community in Paris and that he was in touch with French artists. He also saw Cardano with whom he had worked on lithography in Madrid and it seems likely that his stay in Paris renewed his interest in the technique

In 1816 two private lithographic workshops were successfully established in Paris, by Charles de Lasteyrie and Godefroy Engelmann, and the technique was developed with their help by artists such as Charlet, Devéria, Lami, Carle and Horace Vernet and above all Géricault. Géricault died in 1824, the year of Goya's visit to Paris, when for the first time the Salon exhibition, which opened just before Goya's departure for Bordeaux, included a special section for lithography. It seems probable that Goya visited the Salon and he must certainly have been aware of the latest developments and possibilities of lithography as it was practised in France.

On 1 September Goya was back in Bordeaux where he was joined by his companion Leocadia Weiss and her two younger children, Guillermo and María del Rosario, known as Mariquita, who is now generally thought to have been Goya's child and for whom he always expressed the most touching affection and admiration. They took lodgings and settled down for the winter in the city which, like Paris, was the home of many Spanish emigrés and where Goya, according to his friend Moratín, was quite happy although he missed his son and grandson who had remained in Madrid. He was full of ideas for work and during that first winter made a remarkable series of miniature paintings on ivory in an entirely original technique which he described as 'more like the brushwork of Velasquez than of Mengs'. Throughout his last years in Bordeaux he drew ceaselessly, filling two final albums with drawings which recall many of his earlier themes or record customs, carriages and fairground figures observed in Paris and Bordeaux. In the drawing-book known as Album G, which was probably begun almost as soon as Goya was settled in Bordeaux, a group of drawings on pages 24 to 32, showing curious methods of transport (sedan chairs, a wheelbarrow-carriage, a beggar's cart and skates), is followed immediately on pages 33 to 45 by a series of *locos*, 'lunatics'. Several of them

93 *Modern duel*

96 have suggestive, semi-descriptive titles but page 39, now in the British Museum, is entitled simply *Locos*. It shows a grinning figure, with his jacket apparently pulled up over his head, straddling a crouching man who resembles an animal, while a third figure peers through from behind. Drawn in black chalk, the free, lightly-traced outlines still visible around the main figure were worked over until the design took shape. Stronger strokes define an outline or, more characteristically, create vibrant, zigzag accents or suggest the passage of a form from light to shade. The whole effect is impressionistic and intensely vital, the stance of the leering figure balanced by his side-long glance and outstretched hands which increase the sense of demonic life in the madman. A later drawing in this album is related to one of Goya's lithographs and Goya probably started working in lithography shortly after his arrival in Bordeaux.

He was fortunate in finding an expert French lithographer, called Gaulon, who had opened a lithographic printing works in Bordeaux in 1818. Gaulon encouraged the artist to work directly on the stone, using a scraper to obtain highlights and model the dark areas, a method which Géricault and Delacroix used to brilliant effect. Possibly one of
91 Goya's last lithographs made in Madrid or first in Bordeaux is a small scene with a woman reading to two children in a dark room. Goya's portrayal of the children's rapt attention and of the tranquil, comely figure of the young woman suggests that it was a scene observed in his own home and records his Doña Leocadia and her two children. Although the area of darkest shadow lacks definition, the drawing of the children and the scratched lines which model the woman's dress are already characteristic of the lithographic methods which Goya was to develop and which were described, in a book published in 1858, from the first-hand account of a young Spanish artist, Antonio Brugada, who spent much time with Goya in Bordeaux. 'The artist worked at his lithographs on an easel, the stone placed like a canvas. He handled his crayons like brushes and never sharpened them. He remained standing, walking backwards and forwards every other minute to judge his effects. Usually he covered the whole stone with a uniform grey tone and then removed with the scraper those parts which were to appear light: here a head, a figure; there a horse, a bull. Next the crayon was again employed to strengthen the shadows, the accents, or to indicate the figures and give them movement . . . all Goya's lithographs were executed with a magnifying glass . . . not in order to do very detailed work but because his eyesight was failing.'

During his years in Bordeaux, Goya was preoccupied with the problems of looking after himself and his 'family' there, without depriving his son and grandson of their inheritance. He worried over each renewal of his leave of absence, on which he depended for the continuing payment of his salary as Court Painter, and feared that his fate might be that of Titian, 'to live to be 99 years old and have no other means of support'. These preoccupations were no doubt an additional spur to his projects to publish prints in France. With the help of Gaulon, of whom he made a superb lithographic portrait, Goya
94–5 planned and executed a set of four large lithographs of bullfights, known as the *Bulls of Bordeaux*. A preliminary lithograph, which Goya must have rejected and which is known only from a unique impression (in the Museum in Bordeaux), is signed and dated *Bodeaux* [*sic*] *1825*. The edition of a hundred impressions of each 'course de taureaux' was registered by Gaulon in November and December that year. At the beginning of December, Goya wrote to his friend Joaquín Ferrer in Paris, sending him 'a lithographic
94 proof of a fight with young bulls' (which must refer to the print entitled *Dibersion de España*, 'Spanish entertainment'), 'so that you and our friend Cardano should see it and if you thought some could be sold, I would send as many as you would like . . . I beg you to let me know because I have ready three more of the same size and subject of bulls'.

94 *Spanish entertainment (Bulls of Bordeaux)*

95 *Bullfight in a divided ring (Bulls of Bordeaux)*

96 *Madmen*, drawing from Album G

97 *The blind singer*

98 *Old man on a swing*

99 *A Maja*

Ferrer's reply was evidently not encouraging and the remarks which applied to the lack of success of Goya's bullfight etchings in Madrid in 1816 apply equally to these lithographs in the context of the Paris art market some ten years later. Not even the 'art connoisseurs which abound in that great capital', whom Goya hoped would see his lithographs, could have been expected to appreciate these magnificently impetuous, unpolished works which anticipate the lithographs of Manet in the 1860s and 1870s and are so far in spirit from the wild but essentially elegant romanticism of Delacroix's prints of the later 1820s and even farther from the correct draughtsmanship and good taste which characterised most of the lithographic productions of that period. The verve and brio with which Goya worked on the stones is evident in the numerous alterations which are visible, and in his brilliant use of the scraper to model the figures and add vivid highlights.

Two of the lithographs are untitled and two have a title in Spanish, the *Dibersion de España*, which recalls the title *Barbara diversion* on the frontispiece etching in Ceán's copy of the *Tauromaquia*, and *El famoso Americano, Mariano Ceballos*, the lithograph which recalls the exploits of the South-American Indian whom Goya had depicted in Plates 23 and 24 of the *Tauromaquia* etchings. These Spanish titles suggest that Goya hoped to sell his lithographs principally to the Spanish communities in Paris and Bordeaux, and perhaps also in Spain where he may have taken sample proofs on his last two visits to Madrid, in 1826 when he was retired on full pay, and 1827 when he appears to have made a brief visit to see his son and grandson. In the *Dibersion de España*, the amateur bullfighters who swirl around the group of confused young bulls create a circular type of composition which Goya had developed in some of his later paintings such as the *Village bullfight* (Academy of San Fernando, Madrid) and the 'black paintings' in the Quinta. In two of his three later lithographs, this circular form is applied to the whole composition which appears as a vignette in which landscape or figures are suspended on the sheet, without the rectangular setting of the traditional 'picture' format.

As Goya grew more infirm, he would have been unable to continue with his lithographs in the manner described by Brugada and it was probably in or after 1826 that he began a new series of etchings, based on figures in his last album of drawings. In December 1825, responding to Ferrer's doubts about the saleability of the bullfight lithographs and his suggestion that Goya should reprint an edition of the *Caprichos*, he wrote saying that he could not publish them because 'I gave the copperplates to the King more than 20 years ago like most of the things I engraved which are in the Royal Chalcography, . . . nor will I copy them because I now have better ideas for things which could more easily be sold'. He added that Ferrer should be grateful to him for writing since 'I have neither sight nor pulse nor pen nor inkwell, I lack everything, and only my will remains'.

The will to work, however, never left him and at the age of nearly eighty he could still plan fresh series of prints. The three lithographs already mentioned, including the *Duel* and the *Andalusian dance*, may represent the start of a new series of lithographs. In etching, four subjects are known, single figures of an old man on a swing, a *maja*, a smuggler wrapped in his cloak and a blind singer with a guitar. They are probably among Goya's very last works and were made on small copperplates of which three have additional etchings on the verso, variants without aquatint (apparently not by Goya) of the subjects of his aquatinted designs. The prints are more or less directly based on pages from the last album of drawings, and copies of two of these (one known and one missing in the original album sheets) are in the British Museum, acquired with items from Burty's collection in 1876. The drawings show figures set against a blank background,

100 *Landscape with buildings and trees.* Private Collection

101 *The Colossus*. Museum of Fine Arts, Boston (purchased Katherine Eliot Bullard Fund, 1965)

whereas Goya's prints have a dark aquatint ground in which faint figures and many heads, suggesting demons, can be made out. Two, if not three, of the aquatinted prints were 'completed' after Goya's death (although the biting of the smuggler was so defective that the plate was not printed until 1960). The etchings added on the backs of the plates are closer to the drawings, on pages 22, 31 and 58 of Album H. In spite of their rough and retouched condition, Goya's late etchings, made perhaps only a few months to a year before his death on 16 April 1828, have the vitality and inventive power which characterise all his graphic work from the time of the *Caprichos*.

The Goya Collection
in the British Museum

All the works in Goya's estate at his death in 1828 were inherited by his only son, Francisco Xavier, born in 1784, and after his death in 1854, by his sole heir, Mariano, born in 1806. The undated inventory of works belonging to his son (mentioned in the chapter on the *Proverbios*) describes a vast inheritance of prints, drawings and plates which was sold off by Mariano, mainly to Valentín Carderera, an insatiable collector of Goya's graphic work. Carderera also acquired the trial proofs, drawings and albums of prints that Goya had given to his friend Ceán Bermúdez.

Among the works that came to light in Xavier's estate were the copperplates of the *Tauromaquia*, the *Disasters of War* and the *Proverbios*. A second edition of the *Tauromaquia* was published in 1855. Later, all but two plates of the *Disasters of War* and all but four of the *Proverbios* were acquired by the Academy of San Fernando and joined the plates of the *Caprichos* in the Calcografía in Madrid. The posthumous first editions of the *Disasters* and *Proverbios* were published in 1863 and 1864 respectively.

By the 1860s a number of significant foreign collections of Goya's prints had been formed. William Stirling-Maxwell, the author of the pioneering *Annals of the Artists of Spain* published in 1848, acquired his remarkable group of proofs of the *Disasters* directly from Carderera. (It was sold en bloc in 1951 to the Boston Museum of Fine Arts.) Other collectors were mainly French, prominent among them two editors of the *Gazette des Beaux-Arts*, Emile Galichon and Philippe Burty. They made contact with Carderera who wrote a number of pioneering articles for the *Gazette*. Burty himself went to Spain in 1865, where he is known to have bought prints directly from Goya's grandson.

The British Museum collection of Goya's work was begun as early as 1848 with the purchase at Sotheby's of a fine first edition copy of the *Caprichos* which included a loose impression of one of the rare working proofs. The first drawing, the preparatory study for the etching of the *Garrotted man*, was acquired in 1850 among a small group of Spanish drawings. A unique state of one of the prints after Velasquez was purchased the following year, and the proof of *Las Meninas*, from Lord Cowley's collection, was added in 1860, when it cost £21 – a very high price for the period. A remarkable group of prints and drawings which Carderera had acquired from Mariano Goya was purchased from Colnaghi's in 1862. It included the portrait drawing of Wellington (which was accompanied by an intriguing note written by Mariano and annotated by Carderera), two fine drawings from the albums (one of which had been reproduced to illustrate Carderera's article in the *Gazette des Beaux-Arts*), a number of prints and the first Goya lithograph to enter the collection, the very rare pen lithograph of an old woman spinning, dated 1819.

Five more items were acquired at the Galichon sale in Paris in 1875, but the auction of part of Burty's own collection in London the following year yielded a far richer haul. The Museum in fact purchased twenty lots of Goya material in all, which included the cream of his collection: three of his five working proofs for the *Caprichos* and eight lithographs from the Bordeaux period. But this was at once the culmination and the end of an era. Between 1878 and 1979, apart from one drawing acquired with the Malcolm collection in

1895 and two unimportant purchases of prints, not a single work by Goya entered the collection.

Tomás Harris began assembling his collection in the early 1950s, buying at auction and from dealers and collectors in England and France as well as Spain. He succeeded *2, 43–5, 68* in acquiring a number of individual working proofs as well as the three albums in contemporary bindings which Goya gave to his friend and constant adviser, Juan Agustín Ceán Bermúdez, of which the most important is the extraordinary set of working proofs, with manuscript titles in Goya's hand, of the eighty-two plates of the *Disasters of War*. He also formed a unique collection of almost all the published editions of Goya's prints, including complete sets of the four main series, from the first to the final editions published in 1937. This remarkably complete collection of Goya's work enabled Tomás Harris, through the comparison of many impressions taken from the same plate, to identify Goya's engraving techniques and to study the differences in printing quality between the earliest and latest impressions. The results were published in his definitive study of Goya's prints in the two-volume catalogue of 1964.

In the Print Room one can now compare the preparatory drawing for the *Garrotted* *5–6* *man*, one of Goya's most important early prints, with a contemporary proof and with impressions of the second, third and fourth editions. The working proofs, in unfinished states, some with retouchings, or with manuscript titles and inscriptions, can all be *21–4, 68–9, 76–9* compared with impressions from the first and later published editions, and the later editions can often help to identify the methods and techniques used by the artist which are obscured by the richness of the early impressions. The many different editions themselves illustrate the changes in style and taste of printers and publishers from the late eighteenth century to the 1930s and beyond.

Very few important prints are now missing from the British Museum collection. Most of these are extremely rare, but one still hopes that impressions before the cutting into *100–1* halves of the two beautiful plates of landscapes and of the astonishing *Colossus*, as well as one or two more lithographs and working proofs of the published etchings, may in the course of time be added to complement this magnificent representation.

The present reprint of the 1981 text of this work raises the question of the accuracy of the identification of some of the states or editions of the prints, since much new material has come to light over the years since the publication of Harris's catalogue. Since there is no single, coherent presentation of the new findings, and since these affect only a very small number of works in the list, the descriptions remain unchanged.

GOYA: Complete list of work in British Museum

All works from the Harris collection have inventory numbers beginning 1975-10-25, although the collection was only formally allocated in 1979.

References are to Tomás Harris, *Goya. Engravings and Lithographs*, volume 2.

1	I		Flight into Egypt	1975-10-25-10
3	I	1	San Francisco de Paula	1869-4-10-1643
3	I	2	San Francisco de Paula	1975-10-25-11
3	III	1	San Francisco de Paula	1975-10-25-12
3	III	2	San Francisco de Paula	1975-10-25-13
4	III	1	Los Borrachos	1862-7-12-178
4	III	3	Los Borrachos	1975-10-25-14
5	III	1	Felipe III	1869-4-10-125
5	III	2	Felipe III	1975-10-25-15
6	III	1	Margarita de Austria	1869-4-10-127
7	III	1	Felipe IV	1869-4-10-126
7	III	?	Felipe IV (between 1 and 2)	1975-10-25-16
7	III	2	Felipe IV	1975-10-25-17
7	III	3	Felipe IV	1975-10-25-18
8	III	1	Isabel de Borbón	1869-4-10-128
8	III	2	Isabel de Borbón	1975-10-25-19
9	I	2	Baltasar Carlos (on verso of TH 13 1 1)	1857-6-13-326
9	III	1	Baltasar Carlos	1848-12-9-90
9	III	1	Baltasar Carlos	1882-3-11-46
10	III	1	Conde Duque de Olivares	1869-4-10-130
10	III	2	Conde Duque de Olivares	1975-10-25-20
10	III	3	Conde Duque de Olivares	1975-10-25-21
11	I	4	Infante Don Fernando	1851-12-13-19
11	III	1	Infante Don Fernando	1848-11-25-236
11	III	1	Infante Don Fernando	1851-12-13-18
11	III	?	Infante Don Fernando (between 1 and 2)	1975-10-25-22
11	III	3	Infante Don Fernando	1975-10-25-23
12	I	3	Barbarroxa	1851-12-13-20
12	III	1	Barbarroxa	1848-11-25-242
12	III	3	Barbarroxa	1975-10-25-24
13	I	1	Aesopus (on verso of TH 9 1 2)	1857-6-13-326
13	III	1	Aesopus	1862-7-12-176
13	III	2	Aesopus	1972-9-16-19
13	III	3	Aesopus	1975-10-25-25
14	III	1	Moenippus	1862-7-12-177
15	III	1	Sebastián de Morra	1862-7-12-175
15	III	?	Sebastián de Morra (between 1 and 2)	1975-10-25-26
16	III	1	El Primo	1862-7-12-174
16	III	3	El Primo	1975-10-25-27

17	I	3	Las Meninas	1860-7-14-44
18	I	2	Don Juan de Austria	1860-4-14-26
20	I		The blind guitarist	1854-10-20-17
21	III	1	El agarrotado	1875-6-12-95
21	III	2	El agarrotado	1975-10-25-28
21	III	3	El agarrotado	1975-10-25-29
21	III	4	El agarrotado	1975-10-25-30
23	II		Landscape with buildings and trees	1975-10-25-32
24	II		Landscape with waterfall	1975-10-25-33
25	I	2	Dios se lo pague a usted (in Ceán Tauromaquia album)	1975-10-25-422(2)
25	II		Dios se lo pague a usted	1851-12-13-21
25	III	1	Dios se lo pague a usted	1975-10-25-34
25	III	2	Dios se lo pague a usted	1975-10-25-35
25	IV		Dios se lo pague a usted (impressions on four different papers)	1975-10-25-36 to 39
26	I	2	Tan bárbara la seguridad . . . (in Ceán Desastres album)	1975-10-25-421(87)
26	II	2	Tan bárbara la seguridad . . .	1875-6-12-97
26	III	1	Tan bárbara la seguridad . . .	1975-10-25-40
26	IV		Tan bárbara la seguridad . . . (impressions on three different papers)	1975-10-25-41 to 43
27	I	1	La seguridad de un reo . . . (in Ceán Desastres album)	1975-10-25-421(85)
27	III		La seguridad de un reo . . .	1876-12-9-1095
28	I	1	Si es delinquente . . . (in Ceán Desastres album)	1975-10-25-421(86)
28	III		Si es delinquente . . .	1876-12-9-1096
30	II		Maja (dark background)	1975-10-25-46
30	III		Maja (dark background)	1876-12-9-1094
31	II		Maja (light background)	1975-10-25-47
31	III		Maja (light background)	1876-12-9-1093
31	III		Maja (light background)	1876-5-10-351
32	II		Old man on a swing	1975-10-25-48
32	III		Old man on a swing	1876-12-9-1091
33	II		Old woman on a swing	1975-10-25-51
33	III		Old woman on a swing	1876-12-9-1092
34	II		El embozado	1975-10-25-53
34	III		El embozado	1877-1-13-382
35	II		The blind singer	1875-6-12-96
35	III	1	The blind singer	1975-10-25-54
35	III	2	The blind singer (impressions on three different papers)	1975-10-25-55 to 57
35	III	3	The blind singer	1975-10-25-58

THE CAPRICHOS: Harris 36–115

COMPLETE SETS

II	1	Ceán Bermúdez album	1975-10-25-420(1-85)
II	1	ex-Guiot set, disbound and mounted	1975-10-25-(various)
II	2		1975-10-25-387(1-80)
III	1		1848-7-21-1 to 80
III	2		1975-10-25-388(1-80)
III	3		1975-10-25-389(1-80)
III	5	in modern binding	1975-10-25-390(1-80)
III	5	in original pasteboard covers	1975-10-25-391(1-80)
III	6		1975-10-25-392(1-80)
III	9		1975-10-25-393(1-80)
III	10		1975-10-25-394(1-80)
III	12		1975-10-25-395(1-80)

WORKING AND TRIAL PROOFS

38	I	2	Que viene el Coco (Plate 3)	1876-5-10-313
56	II	1	Qual la descañonan! (Plate 21)	1975-10-25-88
66	I	2	Ruega por ella (Plate 31)	1876-11-11-333
67	I		Por que fue sensible (Plate 32)	1876-11-11-334
80	II		Mucho hay que chupar (Plate 45) (before scratch)	1975-10-25-127
93	I	2	Tragala perro (Plate 58)	1975-10-25-151
97	II	1a	Quien lo creyera! (Plate 62)	1975-10-25-157
103	I	2	Linda maestra! (Plate 68)	1848-7-21-81
-			Copies of Goya's explanatory notes now in the Prado (two sheets)	1975-10-25-432 to 433

EDITION IMPRESSIONS (ALL FROM THE HARRIS COLLECTION)
From the first edition: Harris 102, 111
From the second edition: Harris 36, 38, 39, 67, 83, 98, 104
From the third edition: Harris 82, 83, 98, 104
From the fourth edition: Harris 45, 49, 51, 61, 65, 66, 67, 69, 70, 75, 79, 80, 84, 102, 115
From uncertain editions: Harris 76, 89, 94, 99, 101, 105
From the tenth edition: Harris 38, 39, 68, 69, 71, 77, 88, 90, 91, 92, 108, 110, 113

THE DISASTERS OF WAR: Harris 121–202

COMPLETE SETS

I		Ceán Bermúdez album which includes plates 81 and 82; with pencilled titles by Goya, with manuscript title-page, and with Harris 26–28 inserted at end of volume	1975-10-25-421(1-87)
III	1a	Before all corrections, disbound and mounted	1975-10-25-(various)

III	1a	Before correction of Plate 9	1865-5-20-1151 to 1230
III	1a	Before correction of Plate 9, on thick wove paper	1975-10-25-396(1-80)
III	1b	After all corrections	1975-10-25-397(1-80)
III	2		1975-10-25-398(1-80)
III	3		1975-10-25-399(1-80)
III	4	With undated title-page	1975-10-25-400(1-80)
III	4	With title-page dated 1863	1975-10-25-401(1-80)
III	5		1975-10-25-402(1-80)
III	7	On Imperial Japan paper	1975-10-25-403(1-80)
III	7	On Arches paper	1975-10-25-404(1-80)

TRIAL PROOFS

201	II	1	Fiero monstruo! (Plate 81)	1875-6-12-99
201	II	2	Fiero monstruo! (on Japan)	1975-10-25-300
202	II	1	Esto es lo verdadero (Plate 82)	1876-11-11-335
202	II	2	Esto es lo verdadero (on Japan)	1975-10-25-302

EDITION IMPRESSIONS (ALL FROM THE HARRIS COLLECTION)

From the first edition, after corrections: Harris 123, 128, 129, 134, 137, 138, 140, 142, 144, 147, 149, 151, 152, 153, 154, 155, 156, 159, 166, 167, 169, 175, 183, 186

From the second edition of 1959: Harris 201, 202

THE TAUROMAQUIA: Harris 204–243

COMPLETE SETS

III	1	Ceán Bermúdez album rearranged following manuscript numbering (etched numbers erased), with Harris 25 and 260 inserted at beginning and end of volume, and with manuscript title-page and list of plates	1975-10-25-422(1-37)
III	1	Mounted	1862-7-12-141 to 173
III	2		1858-2-13-4 to 35
III	3		1975-10-25-405(1-40)
III	4	On paper with VGZ watermark	1975-10-25-406(1-40)
III	4	On cream moiré paper	1975-10-25-407(1-40)
III	5		1975-10-25-408(1-40)
III	6		1975-10-25-409(1-40)
III	7		1975-10-25-410(1-40)

WORKING PROOFS

209	I	1	Los moros hacen otro capeo . . . (Plate 6)	1975-10-25-310

EDITION IMPRESSIONS (ALL FROM THE HARRIS COLLECTION)
From an uncertain edition, between first and second: Harris 209, 212, 216, 219, 224
From the third edition: Harris 237, 240, 241, 243
From the fourth edition: Harris 220, 234, 239

THE PROVERBIOS: Harris 248–265

COMPLETE SETS

II	I	Disbound and mounted	1863-11-14-788 to 805
III	I	Disbound and mounted	1975-10-25-(various)
III	3a	With 'Nobles Artes' on title-page	1975-10-25-411(1-18)
III	3b	With 'Bellas Artes' on title-page	1975-10-25-412(1-18)
III	5		1975-10-25-413(1-18)
III	5	Disbound and mounted	1975-10-25-(various)
III	?	Disbound and mounted, undescribed edition, c. 1904, on Japan paper	1975-10-25-(various)
III	6		1975-10-25-414(1-18)
III	7		1975-10-25-415(1-18)
III	8		1975-10-25-416(1-18)
III	9		1975-10-25-417(1-18)

WORKING PROOFS

257	I	I	La mujer y el potro . . . (Plate 10)	1876-5-10-314
260	I	I	Modo de volar (Plate 13) (in Ceán Tauromaquia album)	1975-10-25-422(37)

EDITION IMPRESSIONS (ALL FROM THE HARRIS COLLECTION)
From the fifth edition with numbers masked: Harris 253, 254, 255, 256, 263, 265
From the eighth edition: Harris 253, 255, 256, 264

FOUR ADDITIONAL PLATES: HARRIS 266–269

II	On Japan paper	1931-10-12-4 to 7
III	Impressions as published in *L'Art*	1878-5-11-296 to 299

LITHOGRAPHS: Harris 270–292

270		Old woman spinning	1862-7-12-179
271		Old style duel	1875-6-12-98
276		Woman reading	1876-5-10-356
280		El vito	1876-5-10-362
281		Modern duel	1876-5-10-363
283	II	El famoso Americano, Mariano Ceballos	1876-5-10-357
283	II	El famoso Americano, Mariano Ceballos	1975-10-25-423
283	II	El famoso Americano, Mariano Ceballos	1975-10-25-427

284	II	Bravo toro	1876-5-10-358
284	II	Bravo toro	1975-10-25-424
284	II	Bravo toro	1975-10-25-428
285	I	Dibersion de España	1975-10-25-425
285	II	Dibersion de España	1876-5-10-359
285	II	Dibersion de España	1975-10-25-429
285	II	Dibersion de España (45mm at right not printed)	1876-5-10-360
286	II	Bullfight in a divided ring	1876-5-10-361
286	II	Bullfight in a divided ring	1975-10-25-426
286	II	Bullfight in a divided ring	1975-10-25-430
292		Portrait of a young man (formerly ascribed to Goya)	1876-5-10-364

DRAWINGS

References are to Pierre Gassier, *The Drawings of Goya*, volumes 1 and 2.

G	I	C88	*Por linage de ebreos*, sepia wash, *c*.1814–24	1862-7-12-187
G	I	F54	*Don Quixote*, sepia wash, *c*.1812–23	1862-7-12-188
G	I	G39	*Locos*, black chalk, *c*.1824–8	1980-6-28-56
G	II	19	*The Duke of Wellington*, red chalk over lead pencil, 1812	1862-7-12-185 recto
G	II	37	*The garrotted man*, pen and sepia ink over pencil, *c*. 1778/80	1850-7-13-11
G	II	312	*Inferno*, lithographic ink wash, *c*.1819	1876-5-10-374
G	II	352	*Double equestrian portrait*, pen with brush and sepia wash, *c*.1799	1895-9-15-892
G	II	375	*Friar Juan Fernández de Rojas*, black chalk, 1817–18	1862-7-12-185 verso

Copies after Goya

G	I	(H11)	*Man mocked by demons*, black chalk	1876 5-10-376
G	I	(H22)	*Maja*, black chalk	1876-5-10-375
G	I	(H23)	*Woman with puppies*, ink wash technique and 'black border' as Album E	1979-11-10-32

Bibliography

Reference works, as far as possible in English, are listed together with a selection from the sources, particularly the more recent ones, referred to in the text.

Much of the information on Goya's life and art appears in English and foreign periodicals, in innumerable articles on the different aspects of his work. Useful bibliographies, extensive or critical, will be found in Gassier and Wilson, Symmons and the 1980–1 Hamburg exhibition catalogue, and numerous sources are listed in Glendinning, *Goya and his Critics* (pp.255–85), all cited below.

Many early texts and documents are reproduced, reprinted or translated by Valentín de Sambricio (1946), Enrique Lafuente Ferrari (1947), Tomás Harris (1964), Enriqueta Harris (1969), Pierre Gassier and Juliet Wilson (1971) and Eleanor A. Sayre in the Boston exhibition catalogue (1974) and other publications (1966 and 1971), as well as by Nigel Glendinning, op. cit. above.

The catalogue of the 1996 exhibition devoted to Goya's printmaking, and published with a complete catalogue of the Goya collection in the Biblioteca Nacional in Madrid, addresses many of the issues raised by recent research, and gives a full account of the relevant literature. Some particularly important and useful publications have been added to the present Bibliography.

Catalogues and Facsimile Reproductions of the Prints and Drawings

Real Academia de Bellas Artes de San Fernando (J. Carrete Parrondo and others, ed.), *Catálogo general de la Calcografía Nacional*, Madrid, 1988 (Goya: pp.155–391)

P. Gassier, *The Drawings of Goya*. (I) *The Complete Albums*, London, 1973; (II) *The Sketches, Studies and Individual Drawings*, London, 1975

P. Gassier and J. Wilson, *Goya. His Life and Work*, Fribourg and London, 1971; reprints New York, 1981; Cologne, 1994

T. Harris, *Goya. Engravings and Lithographs*, 2 vols., Oxford, 1964

E. Lafuente Ferrari, *Goya. Complete Etchings, Aquatints and Lithographs*, London, 1962

E. Páez Rios, *Repertorio de grabados españoles en la Biblioteca Nacional*, Madrid, 1981, vol. I (Goya: 949. 1–48)

J. Vega, *Museo del Prado. Catálogo de estampas*, Madrid, 1992 (Goya: pp. 58–110, nos. 238–453)

Facsimiles of the prints and their preparatory drawings published in Spain

J. Camón Aznar, *'Los Disparates' de Goya y sus dibujos preparatorios*, Barcelona, 1951

E. Lafuente Ferrari, *Los Desastres de la Guerra de Goya y sus dibujos preparatorios*, Barcelona, 1952

F. J. Sánchez Cantón, *Los Caprichos de Goya y sus dibujos preparatorios*, Barcelona, 1949

J. Wilson-Bareau, *Goya. La década de Los Caprichos. Dibujos y aguafuertes*, Madrid, 1992

Facsimiles of the prints in the Dover paperbound series, with introductions by P. Hofer

Los Caprichos, New York, 1969
The Disasters of War, New York, 1967
La Tauromaquia and The Bulls of Bordeaux, New York, 1969
The Disparates or, The Proverbios, New York, 1969
See also below under the four main series of prints

Exhibition Catalogues

London, 1963–4
Goya and his Times, Royal Academy of Arts (E. Frankfort, N. Glendinning, T. Harris, P. Troutman and others)

London, 1973
Prints from Spain, Portugal and Latin America, P. & D. Colnaghi

Edinburgh and Glasgow, 1973
Goya. Etchings from Scottish Collections, Scottish Arts Council (Introd. by N. Glendinning)

Boston, 1974
The Changing Image: Prints by Francisco Goya, Museum of Fine Arts (E. A. Sayre and others)

London, 1975
Goya – Engravings & Lithographs from The Tomás Harris Collection, Courtauld Institute Galleries (P. Troutman)

Madrid, 1978
Goya en la Biblioteca Nacional, Biblioteca Nacional (E. Páez Rios and others)

Bordeaux–Paris–Madrid, 1979–80
L'Art européen à la Cour d'Espagne au XVIIIe siècle, Paris (J. Baticle, Y. Bottineau, A. E. Pérez-Sánchez and others)

Hamburg, 1980–1
Goya. Das Zeitalter der Revolutionen 1789–1830, Hamburger Kunsthalle (W. Hofmann, H. Hohl and others)

Frankfurt am Main, 1981
Goya. Zeichnungen und Druckgraphik, Städelsches Kunstinstitut (M. Stufmann, with articles by V. Bozal, J. Held and E. A. Sayre)

Madrid, 1984
La Real Calcografía de Madrid. Goya y sus contemporáneos, Real Academia de Bellas Artes de San Fernando (with articles by E. Lafuente Ferrari, J. Carrete Parrondo)

Madrid, Boston, New York, 1988–9
Goya and the Spirit of Enlightenment, Museo del Prado, Museum of Fine Arts, The Metropolitan Museum of Art (A. E. Pérez Sánchez, E. A. Sayre and others)

Boston, 1991
Goya and the Satirical Print in England and on the Continent, 1730–1850, Boston College Museum of Art (R. Wolf)

Geneva, 1993
Goya | Rembrandt – la mémoire de l'oeil, Cabinet des estampes du Musée d'art et d'histoire (I. Rose-de Viejo)

Madrid, London, Chicago, 1993–4

    Goya. Truth and Fantasy. The Small Paintings, Museo del Prado, Royal Academy of Arts, Art Institute of Chicago (J. Wilson-Bareau and M. B. Mena Marqués, with an essay by W. Hofmann)

Madrid, 1994

    Goya grabador, Fundación Juan March (A. E. Pérez-Sánchez and J. Gállego)

New York, 1995

    Goya in The Metropolitan Museum of Art (C. Ives and S. A. Stein)

Madrid, 1996

    Ydioma universal. Goya en la Biblioteca Nacional, Biblioteca Nacional (E. Santiago and J. Wilson-Bareau)

General Works and Critical Essays

J. Baticle, *Goya*, Paris, 1992; Barcelona, 1995 (revised and augmented)

C. Bédat, *L'Académie des Beaux-Arts de Madrid, 1744–1808*, Toulouse, 1974

J. Caro Baroja, *El Carnaval*, Madrid, 1965

Francisco de Goya, grabador: instantáneos (I) *Caprichos*, (II) *Desastres de la guerra*, (III) *Tauromaquia*, (IV) *Disparates* (V. Bozal, J. Carrete Parrondo, N. Glendinning, J. Gyenes, A. Martínez-Novillo, J. Vega), Madrid, 1992, 4 vols.

N. Glendinning, 'Goya and England in the Nineteenth Century', *Burlington Magazine*, CVI, 1964, 4–14

N. Glendinning, *Goya and his Critics*, New Haven and London, 1977

N. Glendining, 'Nineteenth-century editions of Goya's etchings. New details of the sales statistics', *Print Quarterly*, VI, 1989, 394–403

N. Glendinning, 'A further note on the printing and distribution of Goya's etchings in nineteenth-century Spain', *Print Quarterly*, VIII, 1991, 50–3

Goya. Nuevas visiones, ed. I. García de la Rasilla, F. Calvo Serraller, Madrid, 1987

H. F. Grant, 'The world upside-down', *Studies in Spanish Literature of the Golden Age in honour of Edward Wilson*, ed. R. O. Jones, London, 1973

A. Griffiths, *Prints and Printmaking. An Introduction to the history and techniques*, London, 1980; 2nd ed., revised and augmented, 1996

E. Harris, 'Sir William Stirling-Maxwell and the History of Spanish Art', *Apollo*, LXXIX, January, 1964, 73–7

E. Harris, *Goya*, London and New York, 1969; 2nd ed., revised and augmented, 1994

E. Helman, *Trasmundo de Goya*, Madrid, 1963; reprint 1983

F. D. Klingender, *Goya in the democratic tradition*, London, 1948; reprint 1968

E. Lafuente Ferrari, *Antecedentes, coincidencias e influencias del arte de Goya*, Madrid, 1947; reprint 1987

G. Levitine, 'Some Emblematic Sources of Goya', *Journal of the Warburg and Courtauld Institutes*, XXII, 1959, 106–31

J. López-Rey, 'Goya and the world around him', *Gazette des Beaux-Arts*, XXVIII, 1945, 129–50

J. López-Rey, *A cycle of Goya's drawings*, London, 1956

F. Nordström, *Goya, Saturn and Melancholy*, Stockholm, 1962

X. de Salas, 'Precisiones sobre pinturas de Goya: *El Entierro de la Sardina*, la serie de obras de gabinete de 1793–1794 y otras notas', *Archivo Español de Arte*, XLI, 1968, 1–16

V. de Sambricio, *Tapices de Goya*, Madrid, 1946

F. J. Sánchez Cantón, *The Life and Works of Goya*, Madrid, 1964

F. J. Sánchez Cantón and X. de Salas, *Goya and the Black Paintings*, London, 1964

E. A. Sayre, 'Goya's Bordeaux miniatures', *Boston Museum Bulletin*, LXIV, 1966, 84–123

E. A. Sayre, *Late Caprichos of Goya. Fragments from a series*, New York (Philip Hofer Books), 1971

E. A. Sayre, 'Goya. A moment in Time', *Nationalmuseum Bulletin*, III, 1, Stockholm, 1979, 28–49

R. Shickel, *The World of Goya 1746–1828*, ed. Time-Life Books, New York, 1968

W. Stirling, *Annals of the Artists of Spain*, 2nd ed., London, 1891

S. Symmons, *Goya*, London, 1977

J. A. Tomlinson, *Graphic Evolutions. The Print Series of Francisco Goya*, exh. cat., New York (Columbia University), 1989 (Introd. by D. Rosand)

J. Tomlinson, *Goya in the Twilight of Enlightenment*, New Haven and London, 1992

J. Tomlinson, *Francisco Goya y Lucientes 1746–1828*, London, 1994

See also

COPIES AFTER VELASQUEZ
J. Vega, 'Goya's etchings after Velázquez', *Print Quarterly*, XII, 1995, 145–63

LOS CAPRICHOS
J. Baticle, 'Un nuevo dato sobre los "Caprichos" de Goya', *Archivo Español de Arte*, XLIX, 1976, 330–1

Caprichos de Francisco de Goya: una aproximación y tres estudios (J. Carrete, N. Glendinning, J. M. Serrera, J. Vega), Madrid, 1996

Francisco de Goya. Los Caprichos. Twenty Proofs and a new Census, exh. cat., New York (N. G. Stogdon, Inc.) and London (Artemis Fine Arts Ltd), [1987]

N. Glendinning, 'Goya on women in the *Caprichos*. The case of Castillo's Wife', *Apollo*, CVII, February, 1978, 130–4

E. Harris, 'A contemporary review of Goya's "Caprichos"', *Burlington Magazine*, CVI, 1964, 38–43

E. Helman, 'The younger Moratín and Goya: on *Duendes* and *Brujas*', *Hispanic Review*, XXVII, 1959, 103–22

J. López-Rey, *Goya's Caprichos*, Princeton, 1953; reprint 1970

X. de Salas, 'Light on the Origin of Los Caprichos', *Burlington Magazine*, CXXI, 1979, 711–16

LOS DESASTRES DE LA GUERRA
C. Dodgson, *Los Desastres de la guerra, etched by Francisco de Goya y Lucientes*, Oxford (Roxburghe Club), 1933

N. Glendinning, 'Goya and Van Veen. An emblematic source for some of Goya's late drawings', *Burlington Magazine*, CXIX, 1977, 568–70

N. Glendinning, 'A Solution to the Enigma of Goya's "Emphatic Caprices" Nos. 65–80 of *The Disasters of War*', *Apollo*, CVII, March, 1978, 186–91

E. Lafuente Ferrari, 'Miscelánea sobre grabados de Goya', *Archivo Español de Arte*, XXIV, 1951, 93–111

E. Schaar, *Goya. Los Desastres de la Guerra*, exh. cat., Hamburg (Hamburger Kunsthalle), 1992

LA TAUROMAQUIA
P. Gassier, *Goya, toros y toreros*, exh. cat., Arles–Madrid, 1990

N. Glendinning, 'A new view of Goya's *Tauromaquia*', *Journal of the Warburg and Courtauld Institutes*, XXIV, 1961, 120–7

E. Lafuente Ferrari, 'Ilustración y elaboración en la "Tauromaquia" de Goya', *Archivo Español de Arte*, LXXV, 1946, 177–216

E. Lafuente Ferrari, 'Los toros en las artes plásticas' in *Los Toros*, ed. J. M. de Cossío, Madrid, 1947, vol. 3; reprint 1962, vol. 2

E. Lafuente Ferrari, *Francisco Goya y Lucientes. La Tauromaquia*, Paris (Le Club français du Livre), 1963

A. Martínez-Novillo, *Tauromaquia. Primera tirada. Madrid. 1816*, exh. cat., Rome, 1994

LOS PROVERBIOS – LOS DISPARATES

N. Glendinning, 'Some versions of Carnival: Goya and Alas', *Studies in Modern Spanish Literature and Art presented to Helen F. Grant*, London, 1972

S. Holo, *Goya: Los Disparates*, exh. cat., Washington State University Press, Pullman, 1976

LITHOGRAPHS

J. Vega, *Origen de la litografía en España. El Real Establecimiento Litográfico*, exh. cat., Madrid (Museo Casa de la Moneda), 1990